Edinburgh Then

1. The elegance of Princes Street . . . tram cars up the middle of the road and room for the not too many cars to park. Shops still had their sun blinds and individual character, and pedestrians could even stroll across the road.

Hamish Coghill

First published 1989 by
Archive Publications Ltd
10 Seymour Court
Manor Park
Runcorn
Cheshire WA7 1SY

in association with

The Scotsman Publications Ltd
20 North Bridge
Edinburgh EH1 1YT

ISBN: 0-948946- 51-2

2.The snow's here, so it's off to the Pentlands for these 1954 skiers.

Foreword

The *Evening News* has faithfully and fearlessly told the story of Edinburgh since 1873. Billions of words have been written by journalists, writers and commentators which have not merely chronicled the affairs great and small of the city, but also helped shape the form and substance of Scotland's capital. But it is our pictures, perhaps, which have most vividly told the real story. Tens of thousands of photographs have been published of a community at work, at play, at war and at peace — glimpses of the past, snapshots of history. Our photo-library contains a unique insight into the life and times of our "ain folk". Now, through this fascinating book, we want to share with you just some of those magic moments captured by our photographers over the decades. We can truly put you in the picture about a century of change in one of the world's greatest cities; it is all there in black and white. Happy memories!

Terry Quinn
Editor
Edinburgh Evening News

Introduction

There's a fascination in looking back to what we all fondly recall as the good old days ... the time when we were children, when a day's outing meant a trip to Portobello beach, when the trams shoogled us to school and when the wifies pushing their prams to the steamies were an everyday sight.

Every city changes; once familiar buildings disappear, new blocks rise, housing conditions get better, the streets become busier and people we know are no longer there.

Over the years the photographers of the *Evening News* and the old *Evening Dispatch* — the papers merged in 1963 — have recorded the scenes of the day, from the trivial to the sensational. In pictorial record they have caught a city at work and at leisure, and from their files we have culled these pictures.

Sometimes the good old days were not so good, and things in postwar Edinburgh could be tough for many folk. In these nostalgic pictures, backed by extracts from letters which appeared in our *Edinburgh Then* series in the Saturday pages of the *Evening News*, we are sure you will find a flavour of the city's life over the years.

To our photographers who recorded those times for posterity, our special thanks.

Hamish Coghill

4. The cobbled street, the tram lines, the terrace, the sheer busyness of Leith Street before so much was swept away on the left to make way for the St James' Centre development.

5. The smallest shop in Edinburgh, it boasted. And certainly only one or two customers at a time could crowd into this High Street 'emporium' in the fifties. There were several claims to being the smallest shop in the city, but this one is no longer one of them, having been swept into Edinburgh's past.

6. It may look old-fashioned but the paint department of James Gray in George Street could probably meet most requests from its customers in 1960 — and probably the shop would pride itself on the same service today.

7. The shops, the shops. Where have they all gone? Under the demolisher's hammer, many of them. Or taken over by a multiple group. Gone from one side of Earl Grey Street are Jeffreys and Maitland Radio to make way for road-widening and, many years later, for a huge redevelopment scheme which has recently started at Tollcross. The televisions of 1959 look old-fashioned compared with today's sleek-line versions, but these shops served their community for many years.

8. Princes Street at its height just before the Second World War. In 1939 everyone knew it was Allan's for shoes, Darling's for upmarket clothing, Grant's for books, and Moffat was the photographer. They were the type of family-owned businesses which were to give Princes Street its reputation as one of the great shopping centres of Europe. But again, the passing years have taken their toll and none of the businesses remain the same today. Smart new shop fronts have replaced the distinctive windows of the past, and the street has become packed with the multiples.

9. The Royal Mile was definitely looking run down in 1956 before the restoration work started in the Lawnmarket in Brodie's Close area. Part of the tenements were restored, while the block on the corner with George IV Bridge was demolished to allow the building of Midlothian County Council offices, now occupied by Lothian Regional Council.

10. And at the foot of the Mile things were not much better . . . this area of the Canongate, pictured in late 1957,
has been transformed with the restoration programme which started shortly afterwards.

11. Another stirring parade along Princes Street with Lord Provost Sir James Miller taking the salute at the foot of Hanover Street as the guardsmen march past in 1951. But look at the shops and the once-familiar names in Edinburgh — The Fifty Shilling Tailors with the Brown Derby restaurant above; Hector Powe, the gents' outfitters, next to the Three Tuns pub. Crawford's have moved from that site too. All change indeed.

12. There's a fascination about the pipes and drums of Scotland. Whether it is the stirring spectacle of the lone piper high on the Castle battlements at the close of the Military Tattoo at Festival time, or the concentrated music of a pipe band, the skirl of Scotland never fails to take a trick, particularly with the visitors. The greatest piping spectacle the city has seen came in August 1951 with the march of the 1,000 pipers along Princes Street. So great was the crush of the crowd, many of whom had waited for hours to see the highly publicised event, that the 1,000 bandsmen had to be split into two groups. Nevertheless they made a truly magnificent appearance along the street, headed by the drum majors who set off any occasion with their particular swagger and style.

13. Mind you, these American sailors seem a wee bit uncertain about the pipes at close range when the Air Training Corps band turned out to welcome the United States ship into the Forth with a traditional Scottish greeting in August 1948. Is that man adjusting his hat or covering his ears?

14. Pipers from many lands come to Edinburgh, often to take part in the Tattoo, and the 8th Punjab Regiment pipes and drums rehearsed at Redford Barracks during their visit to the city before appearing at the 1955 Tattoo.

15. It may look like some space age multi-eyed monster, but its purpose is much more practical. The new neuro-surgical operating theatre at the Western General Hospital was the latest in medical advance when it was opened at the end of 1959.

16. And for these nurses it is a chance to learn more about the new techniques in medicine which they will have to work with on their daily rounds of the wards. Principal tutor Miss M Macaskill takes a class in the nurses' training unit at Edinburgh Royal Infirmary in November 1956.

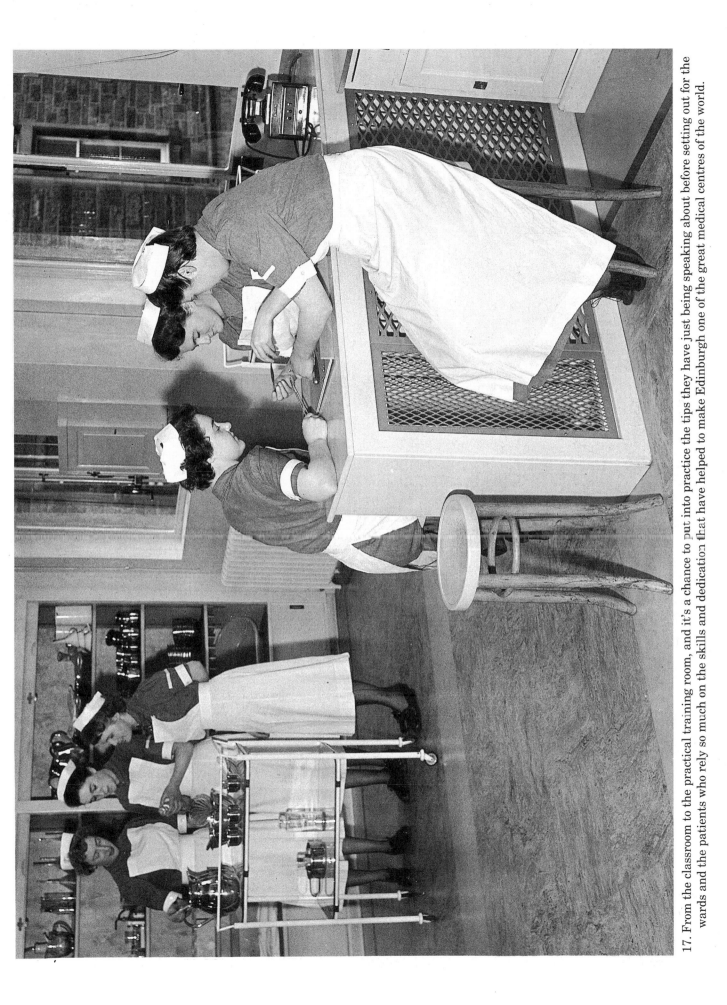

17. From the classroom to the practical training room, and it's a chance to put into practice the tips they have just being speaking about before setting out for the wards and the patients who rely so much on the skills and dedication that have helped to make Edinburgh one of the great medical centres of the world.

18. Two of the ferries which plied between Granton and Burntisland, and for the *Willie Muir* on the left it was the last day of service when this picture was taken on 3 March 1937. The *Thane of Fife* took over from the ageing *Willie Muir*.

19. It is January 1962 and amidst much controversy Edinburgh has started to build its first multi-storey car park in Castle Terrace. It's still going strong today and packing them in!

20. The site which was to have been an opera house, a festival centre, but it turned into the great hole in the ground which is just being filled in 1989. The Poole's Synod Hall was demolished to make way for the opera house which never came, and this 1960 photograph shows what a fine building was swept away before its time.

21. A sky-eye view of St Andrew Square, dominated by the statue of Viscount Melville on top of his column in the centre of the gardens. Since 1965 when the photo was taken there have been many changes to the buildings in the square, including a partial restoration on the north side and big improvements on the north-west corner at the Queen Street junction.

22. The Caledonian Station in 1960, with its distinctive roof and sidings before being swept away. The Western Approach Road now runs across the lines of the track to Lothian Road, and the Sheraton Hotel stands opposite the Usher Hall.

23. The peace and calm of George Square in 1960 before Edinburgh University started their redevelopment programme which destroyed forever the charm of the buildings round the gardens. Most of the buildings at the far side of the Square have been replaced by multi-storey teaching blocks, while on the right the University Library now towers over the scene. Already in the foreground the first intrusions into the Georgian square are started, and further building is yet to take place along that side.

24. 1962 and this is Leith Street as it will long be remembered. A bustling street of shops with a distinctive terrace stretching down to Union Place and the top of the Walk. The buildings in St James' Square are still houses, albeit by then in urgent need of modernisation. But that was not to be — the St James' Square redevelopment was decreed and a shopping centre and the New St Andrew's House now occupy the bulk of the site. In the foreground the domes of New and Old Register House continue to hold their place on the skyline, and further north the bus station has staked its claim on the site of the old St Andrew Square picture house.

25. Another view of the Leith Street area in 1962, with the St James' Square houses dominating the centre. In the foreground is the shell of the old Theatre Royal, destroyed by fire in 1946, up against St Mary's Roman Catholic Cathedral.

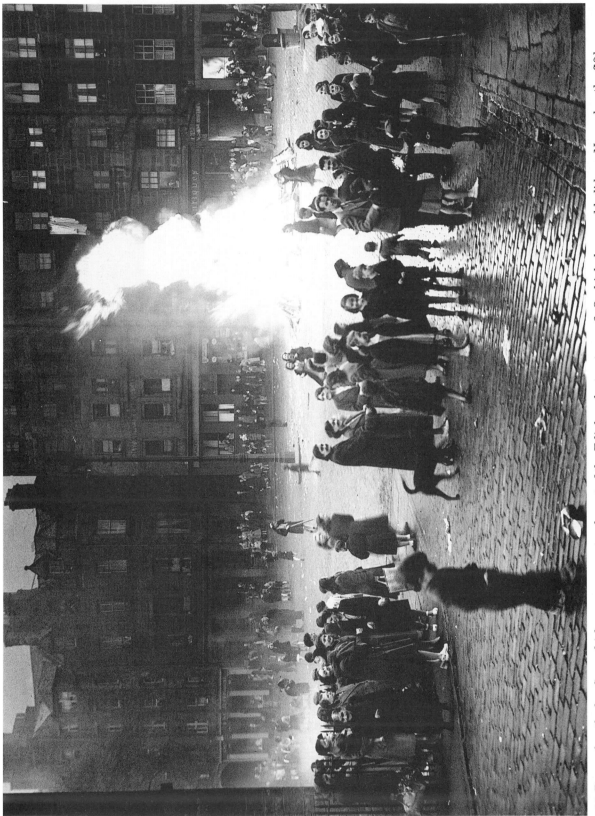

26. Remember the bonfires which were once so much part of the Edinburgh street scene? On high days and holidays, November the fifth, or any other excuse for a celebration, the rubbish was gathered in the middle of the street and crowds gathered round to watch. This one was in the Grassmarket on Victoria Day 1952 — with what few cars there were around in those days safely removed from the heat!

27. How did my team get on then? Eighty-year-old night watchman W A Ferguson ponders the Green *Dispatch* in February 1957 as he huddles over his brazier. The Green and Pink *News* were the rival sporting papers until the two were merged in 1963.

28. Keep off the grass meant "keep off" in Princes Street Gardens in the summer of 1955; and the park keepers made sure the rules were kept. Probably not everyone obeyed the instruction to move as readily as these would-be sun seekers.

29-30. Rowing in the city cente. St Margaret's Loch in Holyrood Park was always a popular spot and whether it was dad's shot to row (1954) or a chance for the youngsters to show their prowess (1957), it remained a popular pastime for many years.

31. They used to pack them into the seats at the Ross Bandstand in West Princes Street Gardens — here in 1955 it was a children's concert drawing the crowds. And if you couldn't afford the few pence admission then it was always free entertainment by simply standing round the perimeter fence.

32-33. The great personalities of the Heart of Midlothian football team were the toast of the town the night they brought back the Scottish Cup after beating Celtic 3-1 at Hampden on 21 April 1956. Celebrating in the Charlotte Rooms that night after a rousing open-top bus welcome back to Edinburgh are *left to right*: Willie Duff, Tam Mackenzie, Willie Bauld, Jimmy Wardhaugh, Freddie Glidden, Alex Young and Ian Crawford. And for the delirious Hearts supporters it was a chance to see the trophy close up — a day all the Tynecastle fans who were there will never forget.

34. Where is he now? A confident youngster who knew Hearts would win in April 1956.

35. Hard at it making the golf balls in the North British Rubber's Castle Mills.

36. There were few better known personalities in the forties and fifties than Lord Provost Sir Will Y Darling, who later became one of Edinburgh's Members of Parliament. A larger than life character, he dominated the political scene and his distinctive style of dress made him a popular and immediately recognisable figure wherever he and Lady Darling went.

37. A curl to the beard, sir? Another of the city's distinguished residents, author Sir Compton Mackenzie, takes time off from his writing chores to lark at the opening of a hairdressing salon.

38. It's 'Wedding Fever' for these distinguished Scots players presenting the comedy in Edinburgh. *Left to right:* Lennox Milne, Jimmy Logan, Marillyn Gray, Walter Carr and Dorothy Bibby brought much laughter with the show which toured Scotland.

39. Now a distinguished Parliamentarian and MP for Dunfermline East, Gordon Brown looks set for a beer shampoo from his supporters at Edinburgh University where he was elected Student Rector. The time is 1972 and the young Mr Brown is now a leading figure in the Labour Party's House of Commons team.

Readers' Letters

EDINBURGH THEN

Oh! Edinburgh how I loved you
In the good old days
When lads and lasses roamed through
Your alleys and your ways.

Down the High Street we would wander
Passing barries, buckie-wives and brokers,
Then the Canongate we would saunter,
Laughing with eccentric jokers.

Through Holyrood Palace gates we'd go
To climb Arthur's Seat for a view.
Then we'd stand in awe at the sight below.
Oh! Edinburgh there's none such as you.

There's our school on yonder hill
And the lochs so bright and shiny
Oh! the laughs that we had I remember still
At St Margaret's, Duddingston and Dunsapie.

There's Arthur Street so narrow and steep,
With Dumbiedykes down in the valley,
There's children playing beside the sheep
And housewives talking and ever so jolly.

Now time goes by I will agree
And things do change a lot
But children's hearts so filled with glee
Are memories that can't be bought.

The Castle still stands upon the rock,
But it must look down in sorrow
As modern buildings seem to mock,
And more to come tomorrow.

But Edinburgh! I still love you
And you must march with time
But leave me with my good old view,
And memories that are mine.

Nell Ferguson

SPECIAL MEMORIES OF A SPECIAL PLACE

As a child I was fortunate to live within sight and walking distance of the King's Park (as it was known then). It was my playground, a beautiful spacious clean area which gave me the freedom to run, climb, laugh, shout, kick a ball about, play rounders or play in the swing park.

The swing park was a great favourite. I remember the tall, strong, dull old iron stands supporting the swings and the shiny black iron bars on the roundabout, polished with the backsides of many children in the area. They took it in turns to hold on to a bar of the roundabout, run around in a circle pushing as hard as they possibly could to get up speed, then, panting hard, jump on and slide along the bar with a satisfied laugh and eyes shining. Each one felt sure they had made it go faster than anyone else. The challenge to each other was who could beam the highest on the swings, and the really daring act was to jump off and try to throw the swing over the bar. The noise of the clanging chains quickly brought the swing park attendant running after the culprits.

Usually it was the same children who at the end of the day ran to the "Parkie" when they saw him collect the long pole with metal hook to unhitch the swings, helping to gather them up and deposit them in the large wooden box against the wall. They would shout as they ran home: "Good night, Parkie".

The changing seasons brought their own delights to the children. In spring the wild flowers grew in abundance, and in summer the poppy hill was covered with the large red fragile flowers which swayed with the slightest breeze. Autumn was the time for building piles of dead leaves and crunching them under your feet, and winter was the season for sledging and playing in the snow.

A mixture of fun and fear was experienced the first time anyone climbed the *Giant Footsteps*. This was the exciting name invented by the local bairns for the pathway formed by bare patches of earth scattered in rough step formation up a steep incline to the Radical Road.

In the summer the long dry grassy slope in the valley provided a terrific slide, and boys and girls alike suffered torn breeks from sliding down on a piece of cardboard. In the winter the same area when covered with snow was wonderful for sledging, only it was old metal trays that were used then. But the end result was always the same.

Easter Sunday provided its own special picture with lots and lots of children with or without parents, some dressed in new clothes and others wearing cleanly washed clothes and new hair ribbons. All were carrying at least one chocolate egg and one or more dyed hard boiled eggs of various colours. It was the custom for each egg to be rolled down the hill until it broke before being eaten. On leaving at the end of the day a backward glance provided a picture of a multicoloured carpet of broken egg shells covering the beautiful green grass.

I remember the occasion when King George VI and Queen Elizabeth brought their two daughters with them to Holyrood Palace for the first time, and I saw them drive around the park in an open landau against the background of Jeanie Dean's cottage and Arthur's Seat. The Princesses were dressed alike in blue hats and coats. The scene was unforgettable: the magnificence of the cavalry escort riding in front of and behind the Royal carriage; the brilliant sunshine highlighting the colours of the uniforms and the swinging movement of the coloured plumes on the helmets of soldiers; and the glinting of the breastplates, buckles, buttons, spurs and shining harnesses on the sleek horses.

My love for this beautiful park has grown over the years. During the war years, when I returned home on leave, I would climb to the top deck of the bus to see my most beautiful view of the city — the natural reclining

40. It's the Trades Holidays in 1955 and for these stay-at-home children there's always plenty to do. The sunshine draws them out for a paddle at St Margaret's Loch in Holyrood Park.

shape of a lion that is Arthur's Seat. It has been my sanctuary when I have been depressed, had a heavy heart or needed to think out some problem. I could sit amidst all that quiet beauty, and look around at the magnificent view as far as the eye could see. The distant hills, the land, sea and sky would merge into one kaleidoscope of colour. Somehow my problems seemed to ease with a feeling that I had spoken to someone, yet not a sound was uttered and no one had spoken to me — or had they?

There have been many changes over the years, with more cars, and increasing speed causing accidents and restricting the freedom of children. Sadly there's no longer an abundance of wild flowers and the poppy hill is no longer covered with the delicate scarlet poppy — saplings have been planted there and on the slopes of the valley so there is no longer the joy of sliding or sledging for the local youngsters. I remember my resentment and anger at seeing the long deep gully cut around the bottom of the hill leading up to the Radical Road. This I believe was to protect the public from falling rocks from Salisbury Crags. Thankfully nature took over and covered the ugly scar with lush green grass. The closure of James Clark's school meant no more an explosion of noisy youth bursting forth from that beautiful building when the school bell rang out loud and clear. Jeanie Dean's cottage has also long since disappeared.

Thankfully neither man nor nature has as yet interfered with the shape and grandeur of Arthur's Seat. That, at least, remains intact — a sight to be loved and admired which has lasted for me from the far-sighted clear vision of a child to the optically assisted tired eyes of a senior citizen.

Jess Rogan

A WARTIME CHILDHOOD

When the war began I had just started school; when it ended I was almost a teenager. However, I always considered myself more fortunate than my baby sister because I could remember bananas, large chocolate Easter eggs, toys and pretty clothes which were very scarce or non-existent until she was nine years old.

War did not mean very much to us prior to the autumn of 1939. I can remember adults saying that it would never happen, although we were provided with sheets of corrugated iron which would eventually be constructed into Anderson shelters, in case of air raids. Against the garden fence, those iron sheets provided us with impromtu chutes, upon which we slid up and down until they were used for their intended purpose. We watched fascinated as they were transformed into little houses well below ground level. Bunk beds, blankets, food, candles, torches, first-aid kits, kettles and pots and a Tommy's cooker (solidified methylated spirits over a metal frame) were installed to provide comfort if required. Barrage balloons started to appear in the sky; we were told that those graceful blimp-like constructions would catch enemy planes in the attached ropes should they decide to bomb the Castle or the Forth Bridge. I do not remember hearing if they ever caught a plane. Air raid sirens were tested and black-out precautions set in motion. One day the children were told to be quiet — Mr Chamberlain was going to speak on the wireless. Dad rescued me from my favourite hiding place under the table and gently told me that we were going to stay in the country for a while as the war had started. Mum, baby sister and I arrived at Galashiels later that day. Dad returned to Edinburgh alone. Two weeks and no bombs later, and very homesick, we all returned home to face the war in the Capital.

Most of my friends, fathers and elder brothers were conscripted for the forces; some did not return, some were wounded and some became prisoners of war. We were very lucky as Dad's job was of military importance and he could not be spared to serve in the forces, although he constantly wished to enlist.

The bombs did come to Edinburgh. One intended for the Castle went off course and hit a distillery near Dalry Road. Rumour had it that local people were catching whisky in lemonade bottles as it ran in the gutter. Leith received quite a bit of bombing and I believe enemy planes were brought down at the Forth Bridge. We worried constantly for friends in Clydebank, who were bombed regularly.

Times became leaner and we planted lots of vegetables in the garden, as we were urged to "dig for victory". Dried eggs, Spam and saccharine were added to our diet for the first time. Cod liver oil and orange juice supplemented lacking vitamins. The absence of sweets and sugar in our diet gave us a legacy of healthy teeth, which are still the envy of our children. Mum would occasionally take us to the subsidised British Restaurants, where a three course dinner could be provided for 1/6d to 2/-. Two of my favourites were Clarinda's at Bristo and The Ark in the Canongate.

Clothing was a problem, especially as I grew so quickly, although I was granted extra clothing coupons because I had big feet. Clothes were let down or made over. A friend was envied when she sported a new winter coat and matching skirt made from army blankets, and a local bride's wedding dress was made from parachute cloth. No one enquired where those materials came from. The whole parts of hand-knitted jumpers were ripped down and re-knitted into gloves, socks, blankets and pixie-hoods for the little girls. Paper, rags and tin cans were saved and recycled; nothing was wasted.

School was a bit of a problem in wartime. Most of the young teachers had been called up. If there had been an air raid warning and we had spent part of the previous night in an air raid shelter, we were allowed to arrive at school later in the morning. Some pupils still arrived on time, some later, so there were days when it took ages for classes to start. As the war progressed it was thought that it might be dangerous to have primary school classes in case of daytime air raids. Local people with a spare room large enough for a table and chairs for several pupils, plus teacher, let out their room to the intricacies of long division sums and the joys of Robert Louis Stevenson's *Kidnapped* and *Treasure Island*.

In spite of darkened streets and black-outs, I can remember wandering freely to Brownies and choir practice without feeling menaced by the innocence of youth, but I do not recall hearing of many murders or robberies then.

When it was all over, there were parties in all the streets to celebrate VE Day and VJ Day. Long tables were set and everyone managed to provide some food from their meagre larder. I can remember an accordion player, a violinist and banjo player providing the music in our street, while everyone danced and sang *We'll meet again* and *There'll be bluebirds over the White Cliffs of Dover*

and of course *Auld Lang Syne*. This went on until the last ray of sunshine had left the sky. I wanted this happy day to go on for ever and, with the optimism of youth, imagined that everything would return to the world I had known as a six-year-old in a matter of weeks.

It was many years before rationing ended and we slowly learned of the devastation to other cities and European countries, whose privation and suffering during the war had been so much greater than our own. I felt so ashamed that I had complained about wearing Mum's old cut-down dress with the padded shoulders to the primary school leaving party, when there were children who had been orphaned by the war, with no food and no shoes and, worst of all, no homes or relatives. Compared to them, we did not have very much to complain about.

It is strange that forty odd years later I still take nothing for granted and believe the only things worth having in life are the things one has worked for. I am still a bit of a squirrel and hate throwing things away that I can use or other people can use. When my daughter clears her room and wardrobe, she laughs when I empty her rubbish bags of good clothes, unused Christmas presents, books and make-up bundles intended for jumble sales, and remove buttons and zips from older garments. Oh well, old habits die hard as they say. We are a generation apart and my generation did include a wartime childhood in Edinburgh.

Mrs June A Hird
Ashley Terrace
Edinburgh

MURRAYFIELD

I was born in Edinburgh in 1914. We lived in Murrayfield in a house with a front garden and a gate that was opened by a pull-up handle just inside the front door. Some gates had notices on them saying "No Hawkers or Canvassers".

Down on the Corstorphine Road was a dairy like a small farm — two cow byres, a stable for the horse that pulled the milk cart, hens, ducks and cats. The cows were milked by hand, the milk being put in different sized cans after it was separated. The cream cans were gill sized with a lid on a chain.

Roseburn seemed more like a country village. One was greeted in the shops by the owners — D Boyd, the grocer; W P Cumming, the butcher; the Misses Kynock in the haberdashery; MacDowell, the baker, whose tall van was pulled by Tibby the mare. The butcher had two little carts which were driven far too fast by the lads who worked Chico and Snowball up to a fine state of excitement.

We also went for picnics to the Braids taking the tram to Nether Liberton, or to the zoo, although there was also a special bus to the zoo with a sort of awning over it.

Treats into town consisted of going to Macvittie's, or Mackie's, where we sat on the flower-bedecked balconies eating delicious ice cream. I loved to visit Collins' pet shop in Fleshmarket Close. Later my father made a pigeon house, so I installed two pigeons from Collins', not a good buy as they were homers.

At Christmas we always went to the pantomime — Tommy Lorne was the dame and hilariously funny. We also went to the picture houses sometimes — the Princes Cinema, the Caley, the Palace, and later the Rutland. In winter, if the frost held, there was skating at Craiglockhart Pond and on the flooded tennis courts, or inside at Haymarket ice rink.

Edinburgh was safe in those days, with no mugging and very few burglaries — yet the doors were often unlocked and the sash windows with only a snib were easily opened. I do not remember ever hearing of a house being broken into. Children were told "never speak to strange men", but I don't think the children were out alone.

I remember the organ lady and her pony, the one man band, the trumpet man, and Punch and Judy beside the National Gallery, as well as singers and musicians.

These were the happy things about Edinburgh in those days, but there were many children with no socks and shoes, and often no knickers either. Errand boys were weighed sideways by heavy baskets, and TB was still common, as were deaths from diphtheria, scarlet fever and other illnesses. Many women had no coats but wore a tartan shawl wrapped around them usually enclosing the baby as well.

It was not unusual to see a dead horse lying beside the road where it had collapsed, and there were unpleasant accidents involving frightened horses.

Very real poverty was by no means unusual with people living on pease brose and bread which the children begged from the bakers. Many a child knew the old jingle all too well, "pease brose again mither — pease brose again — you're feeding me like a blackbird and me your only wain."

Mrs C Johnstone
Hopetown Terrace
Gullane

PHEMIE

I was particularly interested in the letter about the Pleasance in days gone by, as the writer made reference to being sent to Phemie's for vegetables. The memories came flooding back to me as I read it as Phemie was, in fact, my grandmother and, as a child, my own visits to the shop were frequent. I well remember that lovely smell of apples as she opened the barrels in which they were packed. Nothing to equal it today!

Phemie took great pride in providing her customers with all that was good in the way of fresh fruit and vegetables and she would be up at the crack of dawn every morning — in all weathers — to go to the Fruit Market to order for the day. The smaller items she would carry herself rather than wait for delivery to the shop (she used to joke that it was no wonder she was so small because she had had to carry heavy bags since she was eleven years old).

41. Hordes of enthusiasts skating at Craiglockhart Pond: the date is February 17, 1947, and one of the coldest winters in living memory. But for the skaters it was a time to enjoy the thrills of ice-skating on many ponds throughout the country.

I am sure there will be a number of readers who remember Phemie and who may be interested to know the end of her story. She was forced to give up the shop in her sixties when she was stricken with ill-health and as a result unable to walk for the rest of her life. She took this opportunity to catch up on all the reading she had never had time for in her working life, and it was a full-time occupation keeping her supplied with books! She remained cheerful and never lost her spirit of fun — she had a great fund of stories about her early life and some of the "characters" who came into the shop over the years. A visit to her usually ended in tears — but they were tears of laughter!

EGB
Edinburgh

PLEASANT MEMORIES OF THE PLEASANCE

I took a walk down the Pleasance the other day and was saddened by what I saw.

I was born 75 years ago in a tenement between Adam Street and Drummond Street and the place was teeming with people.

Phemie, the greengrocers, was at the foot of our stair, and many's the "pennyworth of carrot and turnip for soup" I was sent for. Further down, Elsie had the dairy, and Jimmy Rodgers was the butcher. Then there was the Pleasance Church, a hive of activity, with the Saturday

concert for us kids, with a 'turn' and a bun. The highlight was the Sunday school trip, when we even went as far afield as Ratho!

The minister was familiarly known to one and all as Harry Miller, later Sir Harry, and Moderator of the General Assembly.

Everybody knew everybody else, but when I walked down the other day, there were no tenements, some lovely new houses, no shops, and what saddened me the most was the silence.

MMS
Bonnyrigg

WHO NEEDED TELEVISION?

In 1920 my sister and I were brought from a grey Glasgow tenement where the backcourts were our playground to a paradise where our playground was real sand. I loved Portobello from the moment I saw it as a child of seven. I loved the house we stayed in because it had a garden with flowers. I loved the sands, the ponies, even my bucket and spade, but most of all I think I loved *Andre Letta's Pierrot Show*. They performed in a huge marquee at the foot of Wellington Street (now Marlborough Street) and for years the summer only really started when the pierrots opened — Portobello was a duller place when they closed. I often wondered what happened to them in winter.

42. Barely room to move on Portobello Beach during the 1952 Trades.

Andre Letta was a familiar figure in Portobello. He was a tall immaculate man, who always wore a flower in his buttonhole. There was also Joy Carol and rumour had it she was his sweetheart. Anything else was unthinkable. She was a fascinating person, and sometimes a little monkey sat on her shoulder. It wore a red coat and she fed it biscuits. She was often in the box-office in the afternoons and if we children saluted smartly and said OHMS! we were allowed in free to the back row.

Some of the entertainers became well known in the theatre music hall. Dave Willis springs to mind and his son Denny, who followed in his footsteps and was just a lad then, and played with the boys and their peeries and iron girds. Donald Peers of *Babbling Brook* fame, very young and dashing, would walk along the promenade after the show, still in his white tie and tails with a swirling scarlet satin-lined cape — eating chips from a newspaper. Many stars began their careers in the pierrots in Portobello, and the message boys on their bikes whistled their catchy tunes. Who needed television or Top of the Pops?

Mrs Sarah Ashcroft
Northfield Farm Avenue
Edinburgh

DOWN AT CHARLIE'S

I enjoyed reading the article about Charlie's Chippie very much. Somehow, it conjured up so clearly the time and the surroundings.

I was a customer of Charlie's in the thirties and forties. Charlie's full name was Charlie McIlwain and he eventually moved on to another chip shop in Broughton Road, at the corner of Beaverhall Road.

I was also a regular patron at the Band of Hope meeting, held weekly in Canonmills Hall, opposite Charlie's Chippie.

Ours was a close-knit community; the people were very hard working and their pleasures were simple. There was, I recall, a hardware and ironmongery store known to all locals as 'Ma Crocketts'. I used to love to go in there and savour all the strange smells.

Down the road was the infamous Pentland Bar, a place into which we children were on no account to look. I

used to think that the Devil himself must have been a regular visitor.

Up Cannon Lane was the 'Christie', where all bonfires were held.

Cannon Street, which was supposed to be demolished then and which has now been modernised, was the home of places like the ice factory.

How many readers remember The Clarion Dance Hall? Or the bicycle shop where bikes could be hired for 6? This shop did a good trade because money was tight and not many people could afford to buy bikes.

But a question remains in my mind about the place: why was Canonmills called the "Happy Land"? Do any of your readers know?

Mrs M Cameron
Easter Drylaw Drive
Edinburgh

THE TALE OF A CHIP SHOP

Reading Jo Dewar's story about Charlie's Chip Shop brought back memories. I too remember the shop, but not quite so far back.

Charlie and Georgine McIlwain moved shop to the corner of Beaverhall Road. Charlie died in the early fifties but Mrs Mac carried on until the early sixties.

My mother (Jessie) worked with Mrs Mac for years and the highlight of the week for me was a steak pie supper whilst sitting at the fire door of the fryer every Saturday night.

Mrs McIlwain died on 1 March 1987 at the age of ninety-five and, believe it or not, her favourite meal was still a fish supper!

T McLean
Colinton Mains Grove
Edinburgh

GOOD OLD DAYS IN LEITH...

I read the story about Charlie's Chippie and there are so many people we Leithers must not forget. Jock Ward's Chippie was just a few doors down from St Anthony's Lane. It was next door to Guthrie's ham ribs shop.

I think Jock must have been a sportsman as he had photos all over his wee shop. It was down four steps and there was no electricity or gas, but an open fire and a giant pan. His daughter stood and served non-stop. Penny fritters — they were delicious — or a fillet supper at two and a half pence. What a treat! I had to go every Friday for six suppers — it was pay night.

Then there was Kinnairds and his 1d pies with loads of gravy. The Gaiety Theatre was across the road and with our 1d pie and a 2d seat in the "gods" we were well seen to.

Kinnairds Hall was famous for weddings. Everyone could use it.

Then there was Mary Rowley and her fruit shop and Jimmy the butcher who gave you two sugar lumps when you purchased 6d worth of beef.

Then there were the victual dealers and the offal shops. Hendry's was one, and across the road was McLaren's which was more expensive. I was sent to the cheap one for a two and a half pence lamb's head but as there were so many people in front of me I went to the other one. On reaching home I was chased back as my mother was not paying two and a half pence for one with the tongue removed!

When I was having my family we had no Health Service, small wages, no television, no Hoovers, no washing machines and not many had bathrooms. I used to order six flour bags for each new baby, bleach them and use them as sheets, white as snow.

Mrs Anne Hunter
Northfield Crescent
Livingston

SPRING

In the 1930s Easter seemed to herald the spring. We girls would be decked out in white ankle socks and sandals; we would wear our summer dresses but would never feel the cold as our Easter Sunday always brought the sun, or so I remember.

Easter Sunday in our house was a hive of activity. Our eggs were hard boiled, having first been wrapped in onion skins, which gave them a distinct pattern. Usually, by the time we were on our way to Bruntsfield Links half our chocolate eggs would be eaten. Every year we would roll our eggs in the same hollow until they cracked (with a little help from us).

After our feast of hard-boiled eggs and chocolate was downed with our bottle of water, we would go for our favourite walk through the Grange to Blackford Pond to feed the ducks with the remaining crumbs in our poke. Usually we would climb half-way up Blackford Hill from where we would get a good view of Edinburgh, and we would enjoy the music drifting up from the hymn singers at the open air Easter Service.

Lillian Olsen
Moredun Park Road
Edinburgh

POLICE

One of the secrets of doing points duty at the Princes Street and North Bridge junction was to know where the tram destinations were — not always easy for a policeman who may have been a stranger to the city.

In those days friendships were made with drivers of all kinds of vehicles and I am happy to say that "then" has not been forgotten forty-three years later.

I spent many a day on points duty there. I have several pictures of the podium which replaced the centre point, but I might add I felt safer when the trams were there!

James Kidd
Manse Road
Edinburgh

44. The date is May 1953 and there's a quiet tranquility about Bruntsfield Links where these laddies are continuing the traditions of centuries by enjoying a game of golf. The Barclay Church spire dominates the scene with the Castle in the background.

45. An Easter tradition in Edinburgh. Hard-boiled eggs, often dyed or painted, were rolled down a slope, then eaten. Primary classes went out to their nearest park or grassy slope to roll eggs — these youngsters were pictured in Abercorn Park in April 1952.

46. A very young Petula Clark is the centre of attraction during her visit in December 1957.

47. James Robertson-Justice, the leading Scottish character actor who created the role of the irascible surgeon Sir Lancelot Spratt, in the 'Doctor' series of comedy films, makes a point during his installation address as Rector of Edinburgh University. He was elected Rector by the students twice — from 1957 to 1960 and from 1963 to 1966.

48. Edinburgh born and bred . . . and proud the world should know it. His name is Connery, Sean Connery, who made his reputation as Bond, James Bond. The 007 star is pictured with Lord Provost Tom Morgan.

49. Lord Provost Sir John Banks met many visitors during his three-year term of office and in 1955 his welcome was to Douglas Fairbanks, the actor and film star.

50. One of the best known Nationalist figures in Edinburgh for many years was Wendy Wood who fought her cause fiercely, winning some points and losing others. But she was never down for long and always bounced back.

51. He was the singing sensation of the town for a while. Teenager Jackie Dennis made an impact during the fifties but his career petered out and the Tranent laddie went back home with his memories of a showbiz career which didn't quite make it to the top.

52. The heather girls are Susan Pardoe and Elizabeth Griffith and they are dressed in Eliza Doolittle style to welcome film director Anthony Asquith to a birthday celebration of *Pygmalion* at the Edinburgh Film Festival in 1956.

53. Kenneth More, the hunted hero of James Buchan's *Thirty Nine Steps*, filming on the Forth Bridge in 1958.

54. Cabaret in the White Cockade, Rose Street, at Festival time 1957, and the star attraction is Terry Thomas, the dapper comedy actor.

55. Their voices captivated audiences throughout the world and over many years — Anne Ziegler and Webster Booth photographed at a Press conference in the city.

56. Another fine mess you've got me into, Stanley . . . Laurel and his fat pal Oliver Hardy received a tumultuous welcome when they visited Edinburgh in 1954, and they wore bonnets to mark their recognition of the country.

57. Maybe they never hit the headlines, but the chorus line at the Palladium Theatre was the backbone to most of the variety shows which played there after the Second World War. These are the Palladium girls, class of 1958.

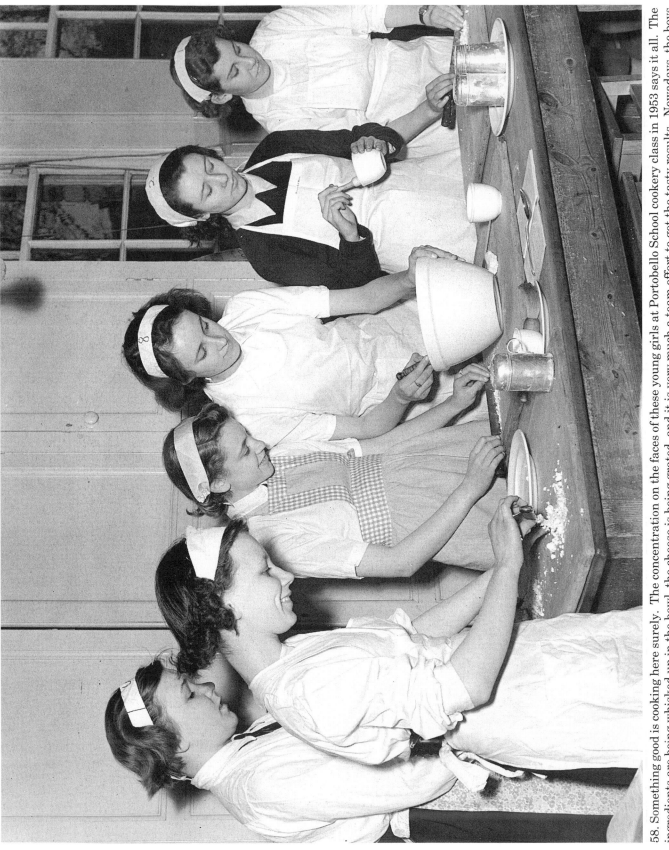

58. Something good is cooking here surely. The concentration on the faces of these young girls at Portobello School cookery class in 1953 says it all. The ingredients are being whisked up in the bowl, the cheese is being grated, and it is very much a team effort to get the tasty results. Nowadays, the boys as well as the girls learn to cook and bake in Edinburgh schools.

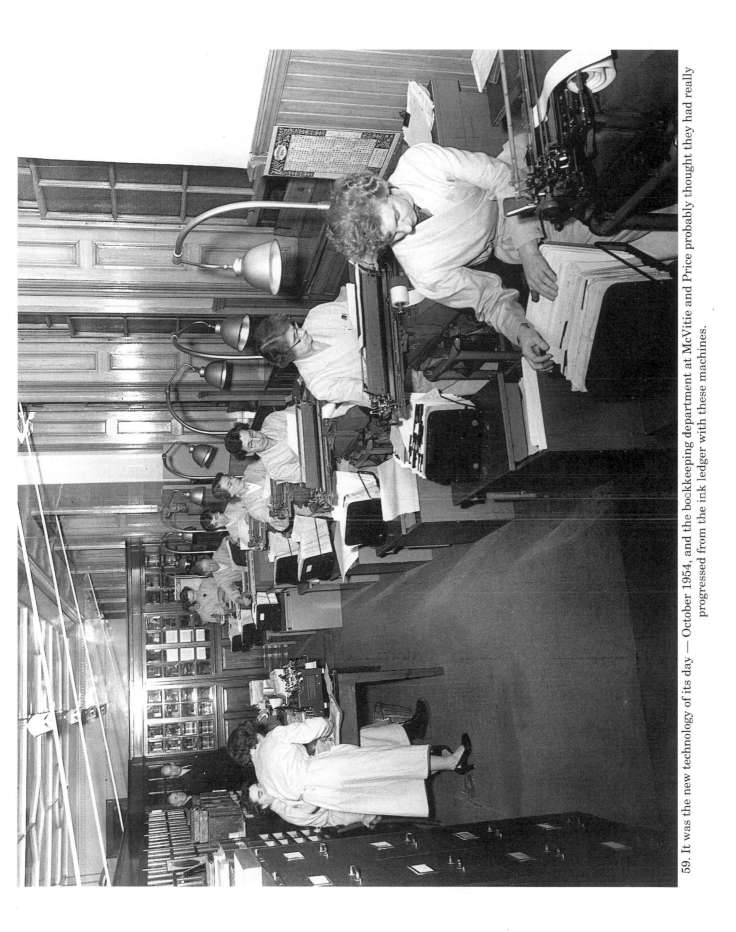

59. It was the new technology of its day — October 1954, and the bookkeeping department at McVitie and Price probably thought they had really progressed from the ink ledger with these machines.

60. It looks very old-fashioned now, but in 1958 this was the way the necks on newly-pressed hot water bottles were opened up in the North British Rubber Company's Fountainbridge works.

61. The newspaper industry has probably seen a more dramatic impact of new technology than many others. The old hot metal days are gone and the computer and screen have replaced the clattering Linotype machines which produced the type with which the papers were printed. This is the caseroom of the *Evening Dispatch* in November 1961.

62. The man who kept the city traffic flowing. The bobby at the West End could easily deal with the traffic flow in 1954, and his skill in signalling was admired by one and all.

63. Another technical step forward — this time in the Capitol Cinema, Leith, where the latest wonder in 1956 is a "Projectomatic."

64. Over to the BBC studios in Queen Street and this was the control panel picking up the 1952 discussion programme in the studio beyond the glass window.

65. Is it exact? These men worked at the now defunct Henry Robb's shipyard at Leith Docks.

66. Sweeping the chimneys the tried and tested way. The brush with the weights to take it down the chimney to remove the soot, the ropes and ladder — they are all part of the equipment used by the city sweeps for many generations.

67. Remember when there were bands playing in the Meadows in the bandstand, when you could picnic and listen to the music? The last chord came in 1953 with the old stand's demolition.

68. A scene familiar to countless generations of students — Graduation Day at Edinburgh University. The scene outside the McEwan Hall is repeated every summer as proud graduates and their parents and friends meet after the conferment ceremony.

69. A packed Usher Hall, and the National Anthem is played under the baton of Alexander Gibson, conductor of the Scottish National Orchestra. It's the start of another Edinburgh Festival and another three weeks of music and drama and other varieties of art to draw the visitors and the townsfolk alike.

70. Feeding time at the zoo, and Su-Su, a new arrival in 1948, finds a tasty bite in the bucket held by Simon Pereka, the elephant keeper.

71. Making a trunk call was obviously a pleasure for the young lad at Edinburgh Zoo when he met the baby elephant. The date is February 1962, but there's no record of the boy's name. Does anyone recognise him?

72-73. The polar bear in his pound was always a popular sight for the visitors. And for many visitors there was no more popular creature at the zoo than Mickey, the orang-utan, who presided as the chief attraction for many years. He is pictured in his prime in February 1954.

74. The penguins at the zoo take a spring stroll in April 1957 watched by an enthusiastic band of spectators.

75. Repair and renovation work to the electric blanket at the Mound in August 1962. The blanket was switched on for the first time in December 1959. The wiring was laid beneath the tarmacadam for the whole 500 yard stretch from the Lawnmarket to Princes Street, and the top 20 yards of Market Street were also heated. The blanket switched on automatically when the temperature dropped, so that ice could not form. But a combination of breakdowns and high running costs led to the blanket being discontinued.

76. Times change and so do the places. This is St Andrew Square at the beginning of 1953. The Gladstone Monument is set to be moved to Coates Gardens to remove a major traffic obstacle, and the SMT buses use the pavement round the Square's gardens as their starting out point before the bus station is built.

77. And here is the new bus station under construction. Much altered since it was first opened, it helped to take away the congestion round St Andrew Square.

Readers' Letters

FORT

My own life began halfway through the current century. Although born at Simpson's I was a "Leither". We lived for the first seven years of my life at 5 Lapicide Place just off North Fort Street. The side of the street I lived in is long gone, but the house had a room and kitchen at the front and a toilet on the landing for two families.

I attended Fort Street School which still stands at the end of the fort wall. The journey to school in 1955 took me past the fort entrance with soldiers still guarding the gate. The return trip from school was past the opening of Wilkie Place — Lapicide Street's great rival at bonfire time with the raiding to and fro of the 'boney' via the vennel at the dead end of Lapicide. It was with a feeling of awe that in 1957 my sister and I accompanied our parents on a trip on the bus, which seemed to take ages. The destination, 11 Muirhouse Drive, a palace or so it seemed — a bright stair, long lobby giving access to two bedrooms, living room, scullery and, most amazing of all, a bathroom.

Muirhouse at that time was in the throes of construction, the tenement just behind ours was still being worked on and as you progressed down the Drive you went from almost complete to foundations of later-to-be-built tenements.

But what freedom! Out the back green door and across the other side of the tarmac drying green, over an old collapsed wire fence and the gone-to-seed fields, with nothing save a low drystane dyke halfway across to stop you walking in a straight line to the railway line to Davidson's Mains, still used at that time to serve the coal yard where Safeway now stands.

In the other direction, using the road up between the 'prefabs' and the 'maisonettes', it was over the dual carriageway, down the side of Salvesen's houses and the access to the beach. A magical place where my pals and I spent our youth covering every inch from the 'white wall' at Gypsy Brae (a great place to swim in the summer) along to the Almond with the choice between going up to the waterfall or out at low tide to Cramond Island — happy days!

Muirhouse in 1957-58 didn't have a school in the scheme so I attended Pennywell School, a collection of long low huts with corrugated roofs, and I hated it.

My mother then took me to Wardie School in Granton Road, where I was enrolled in 1958, and for the next four years I 'commuted' to school. I used a 2d transfer on the No 17 single-decker bus to its terminus in the centre of Granton Square, and often had to leap off before the bus had fully stopped to race across to catch the No 10 before it left to pull up the long hill into Granton Road proper.

Eventually the No 8 bus was extended to terminate at Silverknowes which made travelling slightly easier, but on reflection it was still a long day.

Memories of Wardie linger longest. My teacher was Mrs Horsburgh who taught us for three years, then Mr Cooper who guided us through to the Qualifications. Mr Cooper and Mr Wallace also ran the football teams, guiding us to our greatest success winning the Mackie Shield jointly in 1962.

My hobby during these years was train spotting. Every Tuesday my fellow train spotters and I would catch the No 8 bus up to Leith Street, get off and run full pelt down past the post office sorting office and up over the bridge into Waverley just to catch the engine which would be pulling the 4.05 *Flying Scotsman* from platform 1. We spent hours standing in draughty Waverley or the Caledonian Station on Saturdays just to 'spot' a couple of engines, but it was worth it to see the huge green or red steam engines pull in or out.

My education continued into secondary school with attendance at Ainslie Park, although our class number 1A1 carried the suffix X to identify the fact that we would be attending the nearly complete Craigroyston Secondary School in 1963. It was a strange experience to attend a brand new school where, as second years, we were the oldest pupils and half the school was empty. The rising fortunes in 1963 of the Beatles and the Rolling Stones meant that we copied their dress styles and I have a lasting memory of Cuban heels marching in time down the highly-polished wooden-floored corridors towards morning assembly . . . it must have made those already there think there was an army on the march.

Craigroyston's main attraction was the swimming pool and PE was eagerly anticipated. Less well anticipated was the morning assembly lecture from headmaster Dr Boden.

In 1964 I completed the full circle. To continue my particular course of education I had to return to Leith Academy to prepare for the O grades but left in June 1965 to begin an apprenticeship. The Muirhouse of the late '50s and '60s has changed out of all recognition; the image presented these days bears no resemblance to the happy memories I recall which always seem to be triggered on a Saturday night when reading the *News*. I often wonder, too, where all my classmates and friends in those schools are now.

Ernest Bain
Silverknowes Grove
Edinburgh

SLAUGHTERS

Memories of the 1920s and the smells of a once-familiar shop at the corner of Leith Walk and Dalmeny Street prompted this poem from M H Sadler, Forthview, Newcraighall.

"It was a drysalters, called I think Slaughters. I remember the proprietor as a tall grey man, grey-faced, grey-haired, and always in a grey dust coat. The verses conjure up something of the nostalgia of the shop, and strangely enough there is now a shop called *Nostalgia* on what I remember as the original site."

Wafted from the doorway whiffs of paraffin, camphor, soap
hanging from the ceiling, tin baths, ladders, rope.
Crowded in the window a clothes-horse, washboard, props,
squeezed beside tin kettles, pots and pans, brushes, mops.

Lying on the counter cardboard boxes full of nails.
Piled in heaps in corners, baskets, basins, shiny pails.
Baskets full of firewood, tumblers, dusters, plates,
boxes full of firebricks, black-lead for shining grates.
But best of all the saucers ranged in rows along the way,
full of mystic powders, red, yellow, orange, blue and grey
with in between each saucer, like soldiers shining bright
little lighted nightlights to keep that window bright.

YESTER YEARS IN THE SOUTH SIDE

I remember:-

Belting down Lutton Place on scooters, guiders or roller skates and whirling round at the bottom, into the old *News* Office doorway. Knucklie along the gutter from one end of Oxford Street to the other (no cars parked nose to tail in those days).

Big sisters and sometimes young mums with skipping ropes or playing diabolos in the streets.

Half a dozen guiders in convoy, off to the Blackfords with a billy-can and a quarter pound of sausages during the summer holidays, sometimes at nine o'clock in the morning until after six or seven at night. Coming home tired and dirty after a hard day climbing trees.

Charlie McGaw's chip shop at the bottom of St Bernard's Street with his big greasy fritters and peas and vinegar for twopence. Tony's ice cream shop at the top of St Leonard's Street and his son Tony with his ice cream barrow. An ice cream cone in those days called a "gold log" was colossal for twopence.

The wee shop in St Leonard's Street, where the man would mangle your mum's clean washing, and we took turns at turning the handle of the big mangle for a halfpenny "Vantas Drink".

Chalmer's stable in Spittalfield where they kept the elephants for the circus in the Empire. Many's the time the kids followed them along Clerk Street. Saturday matinee at the Salisbury Picture House for threepence or fourpence, the programme being changed twice weekly.

Or how about a boxing match which was almost certainly guaranteed at turning out time (then 10 o'clock) outside the Castle O'Clouts at the top of St Leonard's Street on Friday and Saturday nights?

Bill Urquhart
Northfield Farm Road
Edinburgh

MEMORIES

What an avalanche of memories are evoked in your sortie down memory lane of the old Edinburgh of our now distant childhoods. Yes, it all comes back — does one ever forget one's early years?

It was a different world — safer indeed, at least from muggings and housebreakings. Maybe we lived in a more innocent age or could it just be a kind of protected ignorance? Little or nothing was ever taught of what is now known as sex education. Parents and relatives whispered things we were not supposed to hear and were not supposed to know.

Thus we roamed unconcerned through the Blackies (the Blackford Hill), often spending whole days in the summer holidays lighting twig fires and boiling up old kettles for a rather smoky brew of tea with which we washed down the corn beef or banana sandwiches we carried.

Sometimes it was through the King's Park, as it was then, to Portobello, for a day with the same sandwiches, sorry "pieces", but this time sand blown, for a dip in the sea, rain or shine.

Princes Street Gardens were another venue where we sported ourselves on the slopes below the Castle where the grass was covered by a carpet of buttercups. It was great fun to stand on the bridge when a train puffed below and all the steam enshrouded you.

Never stuck for choice, there were the canal banks or Hunter's Bog on a windy day when you could not get a breath as the ever-present Edinburgh wind channelled down between the Crags and Arthur's Seat. Then it was up to the Radical Road to gaze down on Edinburgh richly deserving its title of Auld Reekie — who can forget that thick grey mantle of smoke belching out of the tenement chimneys and shrouding the whole city in a dark blanket of smog? I'm sure the Clean Air Act has done more to help city dwellers than anything else.

We were serious, too. Can anyone remember the rather eccentric lady who gave free classes to children on a Saturday morning in the Museum? We were introduced to Eskimos, Egyptian art, pottery and so much more, and encouraged to draw, which I loved. On the culture search again, my happiest memory was of the children's library on George IV Bridge. I can smell the lovely leathery atmosphere even today. It was always warm and you could browse for hours at the long tables, losing yourself with Angela Brazil and Pamela of the Upper Fifth in another world far from the reality of life in a small tenement flat with a smoky chimney and no hot water.

I suppose they were happy days but there were overtones, too, that were not so happy. Working class children were not unacquainted with the shadow of unemployment, money was tight, and it's only looking back that you see how tight it was. There were few luxuries, so taken for granted today. I remember when we got our first wireless, what a step forward that was, even if it was on what was then the dreaded hire purchase.

Holidays in Spain? — lucky ones got a week in Leven or Burntisland. As for the lack of house breaking, it was not exactly a profitable or widespread activity in the part of Edinburgh of my childhood, as there would not be anything worth stealing if you did get in.

Over and above all this was a even deeper cloud — the threat of war. Your father talked about the trenches and gloomily forecast another war, and the word could be heard as you stood and listened to the speakers in the Meadows on a Sunday afternoon. War and rumour of war was in the background and a reality that was to catch up with us youngsters only too soon.

On balance I suppose I can come down on the side of thinking that yes, we did have a happier young life despite the problems of the time; or is it just as you grow older a golden glow covers everything and we remember only long hot summer days? Certainly our youngsters are materially better off but have they ever known the sheer joy of the old games played in the streets, shouting and laughing at tig, peeries, ropes, diabolos, bools and ropes? They will be watching the TV or playing the cassettes — after all, they are safer at home!!

Mary White
Balfour Street
Edinburgh

NIPPERS OF SKIN STREET

In the 1920s and early 1930s, Skin Street was a derogatory pseudonym — used mainly by those who did not live there — for Wardlaw Place, in Gorgie.

Leaving aside for the moment the poverty, the deprivation and the endemic disease (scarlet fever, diphtheria, and tuberculosis), Skin Street of the 1920s and early 1930s was, for the children of the street, the hub of the universe; a world of wonder, magic and excitement.

The street always seemed to be filled with children and the noises multitudes of children make: the thundering of ungreased ballbearings on guiders, the continuous rattle of sticks against railings, the deep rumble of cheap metal-wheeled roller skates on concrete pavements, the intermittent thwack of old tennis balls being kicked or batted and the regular hum of children having fun and playing leevoi and kick-the-can, cuddies leap and hessie, spinning peeries and tossing diabolos, playing peevers and chasing after runaway girds, playing football, kicking yuckers, and playing bools — ringy, holey and guttery.

To add to the cacophony, there were balloon-men festooned in brightly coloured balloons and little celluloid windmills on sticks, blowing battered brass bugles and bellowing "Balloons for rags!" Coalmen with enormous horses pulling heavy carts bawled "Best coal! One and nine a bag!" One decorative coal cart proudly displayed the motto "Rabbie Burns — so does Campbell's coal!"

There were fishmongers pulling carts, and fishwives from Newhaven humping heavy creels of herring. "Cheap!" Everything, according to the vendor, was cheap; and it had to be in the Skin Street of that time. "Cheap kippers! — A penny a pair!"

At least once a month the knife grinder appeared, making the sparks fly as he held a blade against the portable foot-treadle operated grinding wheel. We always stopped to watch the basket maker at work.

It was a real spectacle; a fair, with Indian peddlars selling silks from yellow leathered Bombay suitcases, and fake oriental carpets (probably made in Belgium) which they carried for miles over a permanently drooping shoulder.

Early on Sunday mornings, just before the Salvation Army band tuned up, the 'Soor dook' man arrived with his pony and trap. Then there were street bands and quartets, trios and solo performers, fiddlers, banjo players,

concertina players and virtuosi of the mouth organ and paper-and-comb. There were also pipers and street singers, and Gipsy fortune tellers who were not averse to putting an ancient Romany curse on scoffers.

There was the fruit and vegetable salesman, Ingin' Johnnies, firewood merchants, scrap metal dealers, rag collectors, rent collectors, debt collectors and credit drapers, shilling-a-week men, Kleen-eeze brush salesmen, insurance men, tally men and truant officers (better known as the school board men).

Bookies' runners like Gallus 'Gordon' took illegal street bets as they kept a sharp look out for 'Tanker' (PC Ingles), keeper of law and order.

In the summertime, my favourites (although they could never get me to smile) were the street photographers. Where are they now? I wonder, as I gaze at the still remarkably clear photograph taken outside Number 23 Wardlaw Place nearly sixty years ago.

I remember that itinerant cameraman in his stained black jacket, with his droopy white moustache under the pinched nose of his grey-white face, standing beside the large brass-bound mahogany-cased plate camera, perched on a heavy wooden tripod. "Smile boys — and keep very still!" was his only instruction, as he smoothly removed the lens cap (it apparently had no shutter). Some five to eight seconds later (depending on the weather) when the estimated exposure time was up, the lens cap was instantly replaced. It was done. This then is the final result of his art — this postcard-sized print: a time capsule of eleven boys. In front of the team — a tanner ba'.

Where are they now? I wonder as I gaze at the picture. The Fyffes, the Allans, the Pullars, the Dunbars, Jackie Prosser, John Easton and that little boy — second from the right, middle row — the me of yesterday. And the other boys in the Skin Street of that time, captured on other glossy postcards: Joe Walker, Andrew Anderson, Tom Penman, Jimmy Miles and many others. Where are they now?

Gordon Mills

COOKING SMELLS

Edinburgh Then sparks off many memories for me, just as the smell of new rhubarb cooking brings thoughts of spring and Mr Boni and his tricycle selling his ice cream cones topped with raspberry.

I was born in Stewart Terrace, and how he got to the top I don't know, but every spring round he came again.

Any true Gorgie Keelie will tell you about Leadbetter's, the bakers where you took your jug with you to get gravy for your pies. Sadly another memory came to mind after reading the death notice of Mr Paul Dori who had a fish and chip shop at the bottom of Wardlaw Place. They are now telling us that fish and chips are bad for us. Paul Dori lived till he was ninety-four years old, and his were the best.

When we were teenagers we started dancing at the Westfield Halls run by the Young brothers. After a couple of years you went to the Locarno where you could buy your buttered rolls from Malone's on the way home.

We never know what shop is going to appear in Gorgie Road next but it's fun to try to remember what each one was forty or fifty years ago.

Catherine Morrice
Broomhouse Row
Edinburgh

SWEET MEMORIES ARE BOILING OVER

What a treat to see the old buildings of the fifties era, especially the Ferguson Rock Factory where I worked as a lad as a sugar boiler.

We made the best selling rock in Edinburgh, second to none. There was Andrew the foreman and Lizzy the forewoman, about six males doing the boiling and around eighteen to twenty of the girls rolling, cutting and packing the seven different varieties, which were, if my memory serves me right, raspberry, rose, orange, yellow, lemon, white and ginger.

It was a busy little place and there was a certain pride in turning out the best boxes with the castle on the front. I often wonder what the lads and lassies are doing now.

Come pay day, which was only £3.37½p for learning the job we would buy rock and roll records (the old 78s): Tommy Steele, Elvis, Lonnie Donegan, The Everleys or Dean Martin, Frankie Lane, Johnnie Ray. And maybe the next week it was along to Parkers Stores to buy the American-styled shirts for around four shillings, to match a suit from Jackson's or Claude Alexander's in Leith Street, and crepe-soled shoes from Simpson's shoe shop, also in Leith Street.

After that we would be dressed, either for the Palais de Danse in Fountainbridge, or to pop into the snooker hall or the local picture house (The Blue Halls) probably to see *Rock Around the Clock* with Bill Haley.

There was a closeness in the community among people in lovely old buildings. Just think of the Southside, Potterrow, Fountainbridge, Greenside, Gorgie and Dalry. What is happening to good old Edinburgh?

I am glad to have had those great memories of the fifties, but here's to better days, I hope, for generations to come.

J Heron
North Junction Street
Edinburgh

GROWING UP TO SEE SO MANY CHANGES

I had many happy days as a kid growing up in dear old Charles Street. I lived life to the full amid great friends and kindly neighbours. And Parkers Stores was a second home to us. Every day we would stroll round the store. We knew all the staff by first names and Mr Parker himself was a kind and lovely man, who always had time for kids.

Bored? No way. We had the Meadows on our doorstep

79. Another well-loved shop and other familiar buildings vanished in the big redevelopments sparked by the University's expansion in the Bristo and George Square area. What were the stories of the Woolpack Inn in Bristo Street . . . a hostelry stood on the site for more than two centuries . . . and the other shops which served the district so well? What about Parkers Stores, a higgledy-piggledy shop with a special wonder for youngsters? The date is June 1965, but already the looming David Hume tower predicts the impending passing of this very old part of the town.

80. Ferguson's famous Edinburgh Rock shop and factory with the Royal coat of arms stood on the corner of Melbourne Place and the Lawnmarket. This 1955 photo shows the scene before the whole corner was swept away amid many protests, to build a new office block for Midlothian County Council. Eventually, numbers 1-5 Melbourne Place, 290-298 Lawnmarket and 1 and 2 Victoria Terrace fell beneath the demolisher's hammers. The offices are now occupied by Lothian Regional Council. The picture also shows how light city-centre traffic was in the mid-50s.

and the magic of George Square Gardens.

Saturday nights at ten o'clock, closing time for Charles Bar, was quite entertaining. There was no real violence in the fights, which finished as quickly as they had started.

Then it was on to Lannies for peas and vinegar, if we had made enough money after door-to-door selling of our chopped-up orange boxes, which we got from the store (St Cuthbert's) free.

I have so many memories of the good old South Side. When I see how it has been replaced it makes me sad, but my memories will always remain.

Mrs Margaret Wilson
Claverhouse Drive
The Inch
Edinburgh

NOT 'HIGGLEDY PIGGLEDY'

One department of Parkers that was most definitely not 'higgledy piggledy' was the men's tailoring department, which was housed in a separate shop in Bristo Street.

I wonder how many of your readers will remember this tailoring department which was under the capable and immaculate hands of Mr Newlands (my father), clothing manager there for over twenty-five years. Dad took a great pride in his work, and bolts of serges, flannel, worsteds and suitings were ranged with geometrical accuracy along the shelves.

Dad also took a great pride in his own appearance, and I'm sure some of your older readers will remember him as a black-jacketed, pin-stripe trousered figure with white shirt, starched wing collar and cravat and spats over his well-polished shoes.

In summer, always with a carnation or rose in his buttonhole, black Homburg hat with rolled brim surmounting a fresh complexion, trim moustached and bearded face, he daily made his way up the Bridges to work, never without a walking stick — an accessory, not a necessity. In winter, his fashion winner was his overcoat, a fur lined Melton with an astrakhan collar.

It's odd how writing about him can bring back memories of him standing in the shop, tape measure round his shoulders, smelling of Pears soap and mannikin cigars — our yearly Christmas and birthday gifts to him.

Although he's been gone nearly thirty years now, I doubt if the improvements round Bristo and George Square would have met with his approval. Parkers will always hold a very dear spot in my heart. What a pity one of the new streets couldn't have been called Parkers Place!

M Sadler
Forthview
Newcraighall Road
Edinburgh

A SCHOOL'S TREASURE TROVE OF BOOKS

The news that Peffermill Primary School has just celebrated its 50th anniversary brought back nostalgic memories.

I was a pupil in 1939 and was taught by Miss MacDonald, a Lewis woman who spoke Gaelic and had a pronounced Western Isles accent. Later that year came the war and evacuation and I did not return until 1942.

My next teacher was Miss Gauld, an ex-Boroughmuir pupil, who lived in Bruntsfield. Miss Gauld married an RAF padre and became Mrs Dickson.

On reflection, she was an unconventional teacher. In those days the pupils referred to as "dunces" were seated along the front of the class, with the brightest children to the back.

Mrs Dickson placed her class in rows from front to back thus, at least in theory, removing some of the stigma from pupils with less ability. I never recall any complaint of this arrangement.

In addition to the large box of books which arrived regularly from the public library, Mrs Dickson built up a private library which she expanded regularly at, I suspect, her own expense.

One book I remember clearly concerned a young boy whose widowed mother had to take in a lodger in order to supplement the family income. He was most unhappy — until he discovered that the lodger was the ace reporter from the local paper. This story kindled an interest in writing that has never left me.

I still have a school prize from Peffermill. It is the Margaret Burt Wright award for an essay on "Kindness to Animals" and is signed by A M Murray, Headmaster.

The book title is *Outpost in Papua*, cost 3s 6d (17.5p) and contains 368 pages!

James U Thomson
Midlothian

SOUTH

The reminiscences from our *Evening News* on a Saturday certainly bring back some fond memories to me, having been born and bred in the South Side of Edinburgh, actually between the Royal Infirmary and Surgeons' Hall. Indeed this part of the city in those days, the late '30s onwards, was literally steeped in history.

Incidentally, our address then was 68 Bristo Street although the stair on its own was round the corner in Potterrow. Directly on that corner was a public house nicknamed the Gushet — the proper name being Argyle Arms —facing right down Chapel Street with the continuation of Buccleuch Street straight ahead to Ratcliffe Terrace.

Coming back up Chapel Street there was first of all the hairdresser's on the right-hand corner, either Barret or Barrlet's. Next came a common stair, then an old-fashioned grocer's — managed then by a Mr Somerville who was known for his barrel at the door full of salt herring. There was the very busy post office — managed by Mr and Mrs Duthie, I believe.

Then another stair, No 8. Lastly, and on the same side there was an office of a printing works. However, these printers actually had their machine room based in the first flat in our stair.

On the other side again there was a small sort of second-hand shop on the corner, then another old style common stair. Next came Gilhooly's the butcher. Then we had Harry Main with his wee shop which was anything between drysalter and an ironmonger. On the very corner itself was the wee dairy, its owners being Gillies. Only a few yards along into Crichton Street there was another old-fashioned dairy called Shaw's. Although down a flight of steps, everything was very clean and fresh. Along with four others I delivered milk in and around the district before leaving for school at around 8.45am. We each got our glass of milk and two rich tea biscuits.

Back in Bristo Street, we had a fish and chip shop then run by Mr and Mrs West, who incidentally stayed in Windmill Street for several years before giving up to retire. Soon afterwards the same premises were taken over by an Italian family by the name of Di Placido — where they settled for some years. Across the road there was old Maggie Neave's wee sweetie shop. In between all this were a few common stairs mainly of the spiral type.

There was yet another fish and chip shop known to locals as May's and owned by May and Nello, then a wee licensed grocer's down two steps, Duthie's by name I think, on the other side. Then another old-fashioned grocer's by the name of Shearer's and next door to this came another fairly big drysalter's. On the other side again, there was the Glue Pot which was actually a nickname for the public house properly called the Union Bar. Around the corner passing Parkers we had the Charles Tavern in Charles Street. On the corner of Bristo Street and Marshall Street we had Young's, the baker's. Crossing over to the other corner, there was Whitten's, the newsagent, then Lannie's ice cream shop where with four or five pals we would often enjoy a super helping of peas and vinegar, all for the modest price of sixpence per plate.

A wee tobacconist came next, then yet another public house, the Hall Bar. Next we had yet another family butcher, namely Coghill's, then there was a milliner's shop, then the Woolpack (yet another old public house). Next came Fell's the florist with another only a few yards away, namely Eckford's. Round the corner into Lothian Street was the Crown Bar opposite Brighton Street. Heading for the corner of Lothian Street and Potterrow, there was Ramsay's butcher shop, then the Corner Bar, locally known as Dod's. Coming right down the way to the corner of Potterrow and Marshall Street, passing the back entrance of Gordon's auctioneer saleroom on the way, was yet another public house, the Empire Bar, aptly named because of the nearby Empire Theatre.

Making our way to the Surgeons' Hall, there was the Rat Trap public house. Right on the corner, next to the La Scala picture house, was the Britannia Bar with the Barleycorn pub round in Hill Place. A bit further on into Richmond Street there was wee Anderson's and practically opposite was the Richmond Bar, now the South Sider. Further along there was the Edinburgh Bar on the corner of Gibb's Entry. In between and on the other side was Vert's tobacconist, not forgetting the Perthshire Arms, yet another pub, up two steps with the National Bank on one side, and the Home and Colonial grocer's on the other side.

David Peters
Clovenstone Gardens
Edinburgh

UNIFORM SMILES ON THE CAPITAL'S STREETS

During the twenties and thirties my mate and I delivered many tons of coal to the big private houses in and around Edinburgh.

Driving along Craigmillar Park Road towards Minto Street in the early morning, come rain, hail or shine, there was always a sea of white uniforms on both sides of the street scrubbing door steps or polishing brass nameplates, doorbells etc.

They were cheery, hard-working girls and always waved to us as our lorry crawled up the hill to Salisbury Road where a cheery points policeman waved us on.

Many of the girls in these big private houses worked in conditions prisoners in jail wouldn't tolerate, but they never lost their humour, and many Edinburgh streets seem much poorer since those girls disappeared into the mists of time.

They certainly added sparkle not only to door bells and nameplates, but to all who came in contact with them — the coalman, milkman, grocer's boy, butcher's boy, fishmonger etc.

Passing Piershill Barracks some mornings we used to watch the horses pulling the gun carriages gallop along Portobello Road — what a grand sight to behold, the well-groomed horses, gleaming harnesses and spotless gun carriage. I did not know at the time that when the barracks were demolished I would be delivering coal to the houses built there.

Wm H Combe,
Moredun Park Road
Edinburgh

NO SPACE IN PARKERS

I was born and brought up in Bristo Street and lived above the famous Parkers Stores. Saturday was like a day in Princes Street now; you could hardly walk along the pavement for all the out of town families streaming into Parkers.

Every Saturday, in all weathers, a little old man played his melodian from 10am to 5pm standing on the pavement outside Lear's leather shop.

We used to have back green concerts, charging one penny and dressing up in our mothers' taffeta bedspreads and high heel shoes. Those were great days when everyone was so friendly.

Mrs C Urquhart
Marionville Drive
Edinburgh

GRAND DAYS IN GRANTON

I was brought up at 141 Granton Road when my name was Mina Gillespie. My parents lived there for about fifty years.

Our childhood was exceptionally happy. We used to practically live on Granton beach during the summer, playing on the 'Penny Bap', gathering mussels and collecting partons (large crabs) off the breakwater. We'd walk along the breakwater and swim off the raft.

The middle pier was another exciting place where the trawlers came in and the trawlermen used to give us fresh fish.

We would walk up West Granton Road to the 'Gypsy Brae', down to Royston then on to Cramond. My dad, Jimmy Gillespie, used to walk to work at Granton gas works as there was no transport.

The trams used to stop at Granton Square and when going into Leith we had to go down the Wardie Steps and catch the car to the Kirkgate past Starbank, Newhaven and Fort Street to the shops.

Of course, we could also get the train from Granton Road to Leith or to the 'Caley' at the West End. We had such great neighbours in Granton Road. We lived next door the the 'Store' and we knew all the customers who waited their turn to be served

Mina Murphy
Buckland Path
Buckland
Portsmouth

81. For forty-four years they flocked into the Alhambra Cinema in Leith Walk, where Gracie Fields, Dave Willis, Bud Flannigan, Jack Anthony and Harry Gordon appeared as variety acts. When it closed on 8 March 1958, for manager Mr Alf Beckett it was the end of the job he had held since 1919.

82. A picture for tram connoisseurs at the East End where the tram lines criss-crossed for Princes Street, North Bridge and Leith Street. This is December 1954, and time was running out for the tram cars even then. See the crowds waiting on the island in the middle of the street and the policeman on points duty keeping the not very heavy traffic flowing. Not a traffic warden or yellow line in sight... but the *News* vendor is there outside the GPO. The last tram ran in the city on 16 November 1956.

83. The traffic build-up near Haymarket in 1960 long before the one-way system was put into operation. McDowell's Bread building in Torphichen Street has long since been replaced by an office block.

84. This is Nicolson Street and the attraction in October 1951 is one of the new zebra crossings. The Lyons van is parked outside Ernest Lawsons' sweet shop and next door is McIntyre's, the ladies' outfitters.

85. This magnificent building on George IV Bridge housed Edinburgh's Sheriff Court until it was demolished in 1938 to make way for the National Library of Scotland. This picture was taken in 1931 and the old buildings in the Royal Mile can be seen where the new Sheriff Court was built. The block on the corner is now Lothian Regional Council Chambers.

86. George Street 1959, and Saturday morning motorists are fighting even then for a parking spot. The street, along with St Andrew Square and Charlotte Square at either end, was the first in the city to have parking meters. The picture also recalls another well-known business in the street, Rae Macintosh, the music shop, which is now in Queensferry Street.

87-90. Whatever the season, there's always something to do in Edinburgh. Feeding the ducks has always been a popular pastime, and this wee girl was obviously fascinated by the birds at Blackford Pond. The swans retain their cool elegance on the frozen Dunsapie Loch in Holyrood Park. The ice is still not thick enough for skaters, as the notice warns, but in February 1954 there's still time for more cold weather. For the more energetic it's off to the Pentland Hills to try out the skis. The clothes and other gear look a bit old-fashioned these days but the enthusiasm is still the same and there's plenty of snow for the enthusiastic skiers. There's nothing to beat a birl on a sledge when the conditions are right, and these laddies find the pavement in Holyrood Park just the job for a run.

91. Normally it's the firing of the One O'Clock Gun from the battlements of Edinburgh Castle which attracts the crowds, but this is a special occasion with a full turn-out of Artillerymen to fire a Royal Salute to mark the Queen Mother's birthday.

92. "A wet sheet and a flowing main . . ." These lads maybe dreamt of sailing the high seas in the *Cutty Sark*, but in 1954 their ambitions had to be confined to playing with their yachts at Inverleith Pond. It's still a haunt for enthusiasts although motor and radio-controlled boats vie with the graceful elegance of the yachts.

93. Thomas Wilson, one of the Holyrood Park keepers, patrols on his new scooter in 1956.

94. A young Countess of Dalkeith casts an admiring glance over an Icelandic pony being put through its paces in Holyrood Park, while the youngsters seem more interested in the antics of the photographer.

95. The open-air pool at Portobello, a great attraction for more than forty years.

96. Princes Street Gardens are always a favourite spot in the sunshine for a seat in the sun or in the shade. It's May 1958, so let's enjoy the good weather while we can.

97. Well, these penguins have certainly taken a trick with the big crowd in the Ross Bandstand in Princes Street Gardens. On show from the Zoo, they are enthralling these children — and some look just a wee bit uncertain about the birds!

98-99. Portobello Beach has never lost its lure for visitors and citizens alike. Come on in, the water's fine! The sun doesn't shine all the time at Porty, though. February storms in 1957 make the beach a bit less inviting.

100. It was the great craze for young boys . . . train-spotting. And in the days of the steam engines there was a fascination which has never been replaced by the diesel. These lads are pictured at Waverley Station in August 1959. Did any of them grow up to realise his ambition to be a train driver?

101. Auld Reekie itself. Wreathed in the smoke from thousands of lums and a mist, the city has an ethereal look. Arthur's Seat and Salisbury Crags stand high above the congestion, and many of the city's landmark buildings also stand out.

102. Rattling over the brow of the hill, across George Street and down to the Mound, the No 23 tramcar is heading for Morningside Station.

103-104. Wherever there are bairns, there's a game to play, so it's out into the pend for a runaround. Sometimes the most surprising things come into the courtyard; two girls with their ponies and the lad walking the dogs make this picture in Sciennes in 1959.

105. Climb up Salisbury Crags in the 1950s and early 1960s and this was the view looking over Dumbiedykes and Arthur Street and the Pleasance. The university dome rises in the centre, with the familiar church spires and the Castle in the background. In the far distance is St Mary's Cathedral in Palmerston Place. The view is radically altered now with the ripping out of the slum houses in the foreground to be replaced by new ones.

106. Wartime Edinburgh and these shelters became a familiar sight in many backgreens. Fortunately the city missed out on heavy bombing, but it was a case of being prepared for the worst from the German bombers.

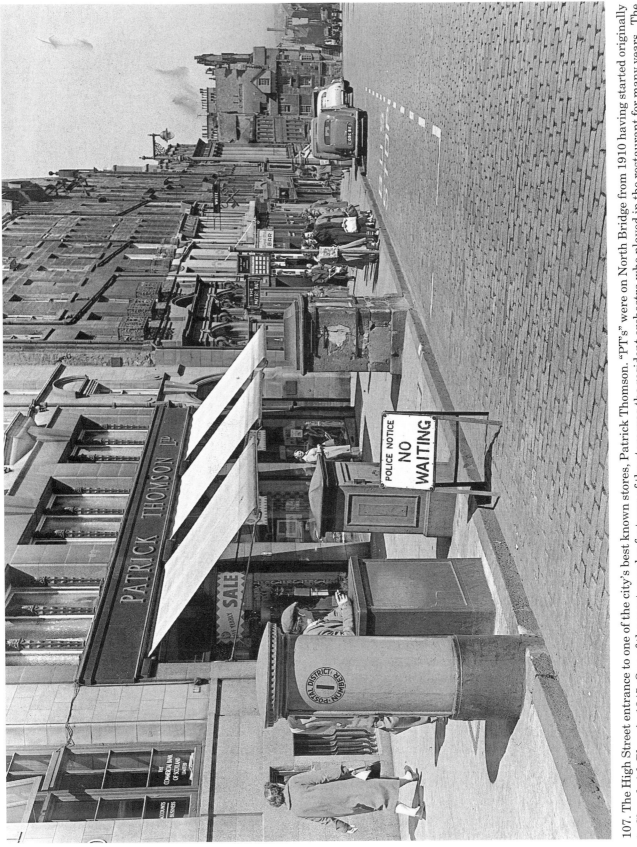

107. The High Street entrance to one of the city's best known stores, Patrick Thomson. "PT's" were on North Bridge from 1910 having started originally in Shandwick Place in 1845. One of the most popular features of the store was the resident orchestra who played in the restaurant for many years. The business became part of the House of Fraser group in 1952 and in 1976 was renamed Arnotts. The main building now houses the Carlton-Highland Hotel.

108. The corner of Queensferry Street and Hope Street in the days when flower beds decorated the street. The double bow-front of the building which Aitken and Niven occupied till they moved to George Street was renovated in 1989.

109. From the air . . . what is now the Morrison Street car park area when it was still occupied by the railway sidings. In the distance the elegant Donaldson's Hospital building stands proud in its own grounds and a much less congested Haymarket is in the centre of the picture.

110. The sweep of the New Town crescents which have given Edinburgh a world-wide reputation for elegant architecture. Looking across the Dean Bridge, Randolph Crescent leads into Ainslie Place and then to Moray Place, with their spectacular views across the valley of the Water of Leith. In the foreground on the left is Clarendon Crescent, with Buckingham Terrace on the other side of the Queensferry Road.

111. The Old Town and the New . . . Edinburgh from the air in 1961. The valley, formerly filled by the waters of the Nor' Loch, is now used for the Waverley Station with the North British Hotel rising above it, and the art galleries at the Mound. The spine of the Old Town, the slope running down from the castle, is still packed with high buildings and distinctive towers like St Giles' and the Tron Kirk. The first streets of the new town were Princes Street, George Street and Queen Street to the north of the valley, much altered from the houses originally built, while to the right St James' Square and the top of Leith Street await the demolisher's hammer, as does the old Greenside area beneath the Calton Hill.

112. A fascination over the years — the four arched jawbones of whales which mark the entrance to the Jawbone Walk at the Meadows. They were left from the Edinburgh International Exhibition of 1886, where they were part of the Shetland industries section. For these youngsters in 1954 they were obviously something to marvel over.

Gilmerton Children's Day

For the older generation of Gilmertonians, the Children's Day is now but a memory and how well I recall that day in 1937 when my sister Anne, seven years old and two years my senior, ran up the stair at our house, 70 Drum Street, and excitedly told the family that she and her classmate Bessie Pentland were to be the Queen's Train Bearers at the forthcoming Children's Day

Anne had gone on to say that earlier in the day a draw had taken place at Gilmerton School. One ticket for each member of the class had been put into a hat and all but two were blanks; and these two bore the words Train Bearer. Anne Thomson and Bessie Pentland drew the coveted tickets so they would be taking part officially in the ceremony which was one of the highlights of the year in the village.

That memorable Saturday morning in June meant an unusually early rise and, while not ignored, the focus of attention was concentrated on the Train Bearer. After all, who could be late when they had to be in the Queen's attendance? But there were final preparations to be made. First, up to Chalmers store at the junction of Drum Street and Main Street (now Ravenscroft Street). There, piled high on the counter, were rows of tinnies (metal cups) on sale for the princely sum of half or one penny — the shop-keeper in a neat white apron did a roaring trade! But oh! those tinnies could burn little fingers. To overcome

this problem the handle was bound with several layers of insulation tape. A ribbon was then attached to the handle and it was ready to be carried over the shoulder.

As the time approached to make our way to the procession, permission was given to dress. White shirt, navy blue trousers, newly whitened sand shoes and knee-length stockings.

The Children's Day was a great day and was supported by all, villagers, businessmen and teachers.

In the late morning the Queen and her entourage, which included Maids of Honour, Train Bearers, Herald, Crown Bearer, Sceptre Bearer, Trumpeter, Scotch Laddie and Pages, all dressed up in their finery, led the procession of children carried on decorated floats, round the village.

The highlight of the day was the crowning of the Queen, a privilege extended to a respected resident. This ceremony took place in Mitchell's Park (now a housing development) to the rear of Society Hall.

The Herald also had his moment of glory with the Royal Proclamation: "Whereas it has come to our knowledge that many of our faithful and devoted subjects desire to know our Royal mind concerning diverse and important questions which affect the present and future well-being of the country in general and Gilmertonians in particular . . ."

Thereafter came the sports, entertainment provided by the band from Dr Guthrie's School, Liberton and of course the food.

Alas, the Gilmerton Children's Day is no more . . .

James U Thomson.

113. The Queen, Margaret Dickson, with her entourage at the crowning ceremony. Others in the picture are believed to include Mary Williams, Anne Bain and Elinor Clarkson.

114. Train bearers Bessie Pentland (*left*) and Anne Thomson (*right*).

115. A proud mother Margaret Pentland with excited train bearers Anne Thomson (*left*) and Bessie Pentland (*right*).

Readers' Letters

BACK TO SCHOOL: HAPPY DAYS

Mary Hawkins can look back over the years and safely say that schooldays really were the best days of her life. Because Mrs Hawkins (73), of Mountcastle Crescent, spent 42 years as a school teacher — the very one pictured in the *News* with a class of enthralled five year olds.

In our *Edinburgh Then* feature we asked who the teacher and pupils were in the 1955 class at Tollcross Primary School. Mrs Hawkins said "A *News* photographer came down to the school that day to take pictures of some wee ones on their very first day in school. He was only supposed to photograph the children but just as he left and I started to speak to the children, he snapped the one with me in it, the cheeky devil. I was surprised enough to see the picture in the paper all those years ago, but I really got a shock when it resurfaced."

Mrs Hawkins spent fourteen years teaching infants at Tollcross. She added "It's difficult to imagine that those children must be about forty years old by now — some of them could even be grandparents! When I first got them they couldn't even tie their shoelaces let alone read or

write. But when they left me to go upstairs to primary three they knew their sums and their alphabet. It would certainly be interesting to find out what some of them are doing now."

117. First day at school and no signs of tears at Tollcross Primary School on 29 August 1955, when these youngsters listened enthralled. Where are they all now? Who was the teacher? What were your first days at school like?

STILL GILL'S BEST FRIENDS

Thirty years have passed since a *News* photographer caught Gillian Penman hugging a dog that dwarfed her. But some things never change.

Gillian might be older, wiser and definitely taller, but her four-legged friends are still bigger than she is.

Our first picture was taken in 1958 when Gillian, then aged two, was at a Caledonian Canine Society dog show at the old Waverley Market.

The boxer was called Digger and belonged to Gillian's parents who bred dogs in Wallyford.

Now Gillian, of Cowpits Cottages, Inveresk, Musselburgh, breeds, keeps and shows her own dogs — seven Great Danes.

Gillian said "I spent all my time with dogs when I was very young. They were my best friends."

DAY CROWNED WITH MEMORIES

One date in particular which sticks in Mrs Jeanette Adam's memory from her childhood is 2 June 1953 — the day of the Queen's Coronation. Because not only did she get a day off school, but along with hundreds of other Edinburgh schoolchildren she received a free commemorative mug with sweets inside.

More than thirty years on, Mrs Adams (43), a part-time post office assistant of Boswell Quadrant, still has her special mug.

119. Two-year-old Gillian Bowen of Wallyford hugs the boxer at the Caledonian Canine Society's open show in the Waverley Market — a well-used venue for such events — in July 1958.

"I was only about ten at the time but I remember that day well because we all got our Coronation mugs and we had a party in our back green at Granton."

The special Coronation beakers were handed out to every child in Edinburgh Corporation's nursery, primary and special schools.

In our feature *Edinburgh Then* we asked how many people still had their mugs tucked away in a cupboard.

Mrs Adams said "I had forgotten all about it until I noticed the picture in the paper. I'm sure there must be mugs just like it sitting in cupboards all over the city."

IT WASN'T LIKE THIS IN OUR DAY

Young married couples today seem to have totally different values, priorities and aspirations. They include various home requirements and improvements, such as central heating, bathroom *en suite*, double glazing, microwave oven, washing machine, tumble drier, wall-to-wall carpeting, fitted wardrobes and freezers.

Fifty years ago such requirements were unknown, though vague references might have been found in the Hollywood films. In the mid-thirties, central heating was a fire in the kitchen which heated the grate and the oven. The hob was extremely handy for allowing the soup to

121. How many of these Coronation beakers are still tucked away in cupboards? Every child in Edinburgh Corporation's nursery, primary and special schools received one.

simmer away ready for the dinner-time onslaught.

The fire itself was multi-purpose because it helped dry clothes on the pulley, or those hanging from a string on the mantlepiece. We had no electric toaster then, so once again the fire was used with the aid of a long wire-pronged fork.

Nowadays, hot and cold water is a must in every home. This was not the case in the mid-thirties when cold water only was the norm. You got hot water by heating it in a pot on the hob; electricity had not yet come into its own!

Bath time for the bairns usually meant them sitting on the bunker at the kitchen window, with their feet in the sink. A large zinc tub was often used for an adult's bath. Picture the scene — sitting in the hot tub by a roaring fire, listening to *In Town Tonight* on the wireless.

Wall-to-wall carpeting was never discussed in those days; linoleum was the thing, with the odd rug or two scattered about. At weekends the day-to-day rugs were put away, to be replaced by the best rugs — "in case of visitors".

Progress really is amazing. It's only when we start comparing past and present that we can appreciate the vast strides made in the past fifty years. It could be argued, perhaps, that we had a 'freezer' in the mid-thirties, only we called it 'the bedroom'! Likewise, grandmother's 'dishwasher' was called 'grandad'!

As for double glazing — there's a wonderful thing! Fifty years ago, in some areas, people were lucky to have windows at all!

'Breakfast patio' would have been another baffling phrase. Breakfast usually took place on the kitchen table, as did every other meal. During the week the table would be covered with an oil-silk cloth. At weekends out would come a white tablecloth, again "in case of visitors".

Home entertainment in those days was mainly the wireless, but oh! what trouble ensued if the accumulator needed to be recharged when a big fight was due to be broadcast. People also played a lot of cards in those days — for match-sticks.

There are so many domestic appliances today that were practically unheard of in the tenement life of the mid-thirties. A stainless steel sink unit was something we saw in an episode of *Flash Gordon*; and a hair-dryer meant a vigorous rub with a towel.

Electric toothbrushes, oil-fired central heating, microwave ovens, video recorders — the mind boggles.

It's a far cry from the mid-thirties when I thought we were moving up in the world when we did away with the gas-mantle to make way for the electric light!

John M Robertson

HAPPY DAYS IN THE CITY FOR TEN SHILLINGS

The picture of the trams at the East End in the *Evening News* brought back many memories.

I remember well Leith Street on a Saturday afternoon sixty years ago, long before Beeching axed the railways. The country folk used to flock from the Waverley Station up the Low Calton to enjoy their Saturday afternoon shopping, maybe a trip to the pictures or dancing and the theatre in the evening. The tailor's assistants could be very persuasive and many a youth found himself being measured for a suit if he stood a minute or two looking in the shop window.

I looked forward to my Saturday visit to the city; they were happy days. Wages were small but we would still manage to take our girlfriends in to town travelling first class in the train, have a nice tea out and spend the evening at the Theatre Royal — all for ten shillings!

That's one memory the pictures in the *News* awakened for me, and there are many, many more. Thank you.

James Dalgleish
Dundas Park
Bonnyrigg

LEISURELY TIMES OF 'PT's' AFTERNOON TEAS

The picture of 'PT's' on the North Bridge reminded me of when I was seventeen — fifty years ago. I worked in the office there on the top floor.

It seems like yesterday when I remember looking over the balcony and listening to the orchestra and watching the capped and aproned waitress serving afternoon tea at the tables — they were leisurely times; it would be lovely to go back to those days.

I also remember Parkers Stores. That was my Saturday afternoon pleasure going up there to hunt for the bargains — I still have a cardigan which I bought for ten shillings (50p) which was quite a lot of money in those days.

Mrs Catherine Roy
Crewe Road
North Edinburgh

DANCE CRAZY

Colin Thomas' article, Dance Crazy, took me back to pre-war years when the Palais de Danse, Fountainbridge, was one of my favourite haunts and ballroom dancing was at its zenith — the foxtrot, the waltz, the quickstep and the tango.

Many famous orchestras played there, including Jack Payne and Jack Hylton after their Edinburgh Empire Show.

The bands usually brought supporting artists with them, and I remember the original Ink Spots singing while we danced.

Hugh Auld
Toronto Avenue
Livingston

AN EDINBURGH CHILDHOOD

I am so proud and grateful to have had an Edinburgh childhood; it is the most beautiful city in the world and no matter how long you have been away, it keeps a hold on you.

Life was very different in the forties, although it wasn't long ago. Bath time meant putting the tin tub in front of the fire, and we had coal fires in the bedrooms when we were ill. I lived in Gloucester Place and we had a key to the Heriot Row gardens — but even the little ones weren't allowed to play ball games in those gardens!

R L Stevenson was a hero, but I don't think there was a brass plate outside his house in those days. One of the very first books I bought for myself was *A Child's Garden of Verse* and I loved *Leerie the Lamplighter* in particular.

Favourite walks were often to Inverleith Pond to watch the model boats and catch tiddlers and tadpoles; or to the cemetery where I loved to practise reading from the headstones! Then there was the Water of Leith and St Bernard's Well which was a rather neglected area in those days; I remember paddling in the Water of Leith and getting a badly cut foot which later went septic and had to be lanced by the family doctor — they came to the house in those days and I don't even remember being taken to a surgery.

I had all the childhood illnesses going — chicken-pox, German measles, scarlet fever, mumps, whooping cough, some of which are almost unknown today.

Perhaps hygiene wasn't all that it should have been, but shopping was certainly a lot more interesting. Milk came round on a cart and was ladled into tin cans, not bottles. The dairy lady was very kind to me and sometimes gave me a 3d piece — riches! Even a farthing was good money.

Fish was brought round by a fishwife with the basket on her back. Not much was pre-packaged and when you went to the grocers you handed him your list and ration books and he weighed everything out and packed it. It probably took a lot longer than now, but you could always have a good chat while waiting.

Alexander Rae was our grocer in Stockbridge and for years after we left Edinburgh he would send us Ferguson's Edinburgh Rock each Christmas (it always had to be Ferguson's for me — do they still make it?). When you shopped in big stores the assistant would put your money into a small container which then whizzed off on an overhead wire to a cashier, who would put your change in it and whiz it back.

We had outings to places like Roslin and Balerno, Joppa and Portobello and, of course, Corstorphine zoo, which must be one of the best in the world. Another favourite walk was to Blackford Pond and we'd climb the hill and watch the hospital patients down below all wrapped up in red blankets as they sat out to get the fresh air. All of this seemed 'far away' so you can imagine the excitement when we went to Ayr or Arran for our holidays.

Games were usually singing games — *In and out the dusty bluebells* or peevers. I had a yo-yo, a kaleidoscope, Dinky toys and a train set that would be worth a fortune now if we'd kept it. I also had a large family of dolls and on very special occasions would be taken to Jenners to buy a new one.

You could buy lovely scraps to make up into books; I think I got mine from a shop in St Stephen's Street. Best of all were the little toy shops in Rose Street, where everything seemed to be handmade. It was the most wonderful place to spend hours in, wondering what to spend your pocket money on! Talking of roses, my favourite sweets were the sticky Rose Buds which you bought in a poke.

Does anyone else remember the 'barrel organ lady' of the war years? We always had pennies to spare for her when she came round. I think she must have been one of Edinburgh's characters because there was a drawing of her in a Festival exhibition once. Unfortunately my copy is now very faded, and I have forgotten her name.

I can remember the wonder of our first radio (that makes me feel old — no TV then!). I never missed *Children's Hour* with Uncle Mac and Auntie Vi and programmes like *Larry the Lamb* and *Said the Cat to the Dog*. You went to the cinema to see films like *Bambi* and *Snow White*.

I went to St Serf's School in Abercromby Place — I believe it's gone now. I remember the beautiful drawing room with its grand piano, Scottish country dancing and being taught how to knit gloves on four needles. It doesn't seem to me to be the easiest way to teach little tots to knit — I never did learn.

We had innocent fun then, especially at Hallowe'en — no nasty 'trick or treat'. You chose the very best turnip to make a lantern out of, hollowing it out and cutting eyes, nose and mouth. After putting a night light inside, then you'd go guising.

I think you only called at the houses of friends and you ended up having a Hallowe'en party with dooking for apples. At Easter you had hard boiled eggs and dyed them. Then you'd take them to nearby gardens and roll them down the slope. People brought up in England don't seem to have kept any of these customs. I pity them.

No memory of Edinburgh would be complete without mention of the trams. It was a sad day when they were replaced by buses.

During the war we were sent food parcels from some organisation in America. I think that's where I got my only taste of chocolate during the war. I used to like the dried egg and condensed milk, and there were always several packets of dates. I haven't eaten a date since.

One of the stranger things I remember buying as a child was rolls of silver foil in a narrow tape. I seem to think it was something to do with parachutes — but then why would people buy them in shops? I do hope someone can enlighten me.

We moved from Edinburgh in the mid 1950s and my last memory must be of the Coronation in 1953. We were so proud and excited — we were the 'Young Elizabethans' and it was to herald a new age of achievement and honour. Where did we go wrong?

I remember that Corporation schoolchildren were all given a commemorative Coronation mug, but in the private schools we got nothing. We had the day off, of course, and the radio was on the entire day — we didn't have TV until some years later. But it didn't matter because you could use your imagination. Also, films of the Coronation were shown in the cinemas within a few days.

The Queen visited Edinburgh very soon afterwards and I waited to see her at different times, at Register House, the Usher Hall, Queen Street and Princes Street.

I remember most the weird silence as she rode in an open carriage down Princes Street when none of her subjects cheered or waved; I can't think why because I wasn't the only one who was keen on the Royal Family and kept scrapbooks of photographs.

But to me there's no place like Edinburgh and I look forward to getting the Saturday *Evening News* which so often prompts me to remember things long forgotten.

Miss Camilla McColm
Sycamore Court
Park Grove
Hull

LEARNING ABOUT THE UNIVERSITY AND LIFE

It was a typical misty-moisty Edinburgh autumn day in 1943 when, along with a small crowd of other young people, I first walked through the imposing archway entrance to the Old Quad.

Most of the others had, like me, only recently left school; most were female, and we had come to fill in the necessary forms and enrol as Freshers for the new term of the Arts faculty.

The war had disrupted most people's lives. Just four years earlier I had been shepherded on to a train along with other similarly-labelled children, laden with gas mask boxes and haversacks, and evacuated from my home in Hull to Scarborough.

After that there had been quite a lot of moving and living in different places, so a move from Yorkshire to Scotland was almost a part of normal life — and yet it wasn't.

We were doing what we most wanted to do by going to university — but it was a privilege, not a right. We were accepted on condition that it was our sworn intention (and we signed papers) to pursue a career the authorities considered essential — 'reserved occupation' — and in the Arts faculty this almost exclusively meant teaching.

There were other rules. All exams must be passed (with only one chance of a re-sit) or you were out! And only women students were allowed to sign on for teaching. The arts faculty was almost exclusively female.

Those war years must have been unlike any others in the university's long history. They were grim for the whole country, and those fortunate enough to be undergraduates then were only too aware that friends and contemporaries were in the armed services or working in the factories or coal mines — where they would be, too, if they failed.

It must have been strange for the lecturers. I recall no female staff to teach all those young women. The professors and readers were all well over military age, and I suspect some had come out of retirement.

Male chauvinism was rife, although we didn't recognise it at the time. An elderly professor of philosophy, confronted

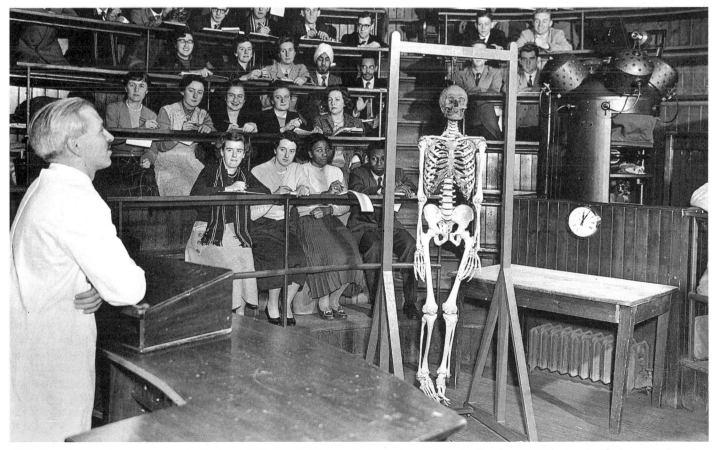

122. Dem bones, dem bones....students at Edinburgh University's anatomy class in October 1956 listen in their serried ranks in the lecture theatre to Professor J.G. Romanes explaining the workings of the human frame. The city is world-renowned as a medical centre and many of the students have doubtless gone on to make their own mark in the field of medicine.

123. A once-familiar sight - an Ingin' Johnny in the streets of Edinburgh. Henri Tenguy is pictured with these youngsters in November 1948. Many onion dealers came to the city from Brittany and Normandy to push their onion-laden bicycles round the doors selling their vegetables.

by rows of young women, began his first lecture by dourly, and not entirely in jest, remarking the whole course was a waste of time because women were never able to comprehend logic!

The war did touch us, of course. My room-mate's dearly loved older brother was reported as having died of wounds in Italy.

I worked during the holidays in a furniture factory which then manufactured ammunition boxes and crosses for war graves. And many of us who felt a little guilty at doing so little for the war effort spent spare time clearing up in the Waverley Station forces canteen.

Bumping into people in the blackout was funny, not frightening, and there was no fear attached to walking alone in the darkened streets late at night. The blackout often made beautiful Edinburgh even more so. On a clear moonlit night the stars were vividly bright and the castle floated dramatically over the shadowed gardens.

Occasionally, in the early hours, one would come across a scene from Dante's *Inferno* as workmen repaired tram lines under dazzlingly bright lights hidden from above by wide canopies.

I appreciated less the necessity for repairing tram lines when I had digs in Morningside Road, for the 'half-tram' — a single decker which carried the repair gangs — would clatter at full speed down from Churchhill in the wee small hours, making enough noise to waken even the soundest sleeper!

Much has deservedly been written about Edinburgh's student landladies for the majority were kindly and generous. These 'dragon ladies' almost all felt responsible for the young people, most of them away from home for the first time, for whom they provided bed and board, and as rationing grew stricter, the board became more of a problem — students take quite a lot of feeding.

I still remember my humiliation when, sitting at tea with the other students, I reached out towards a plate on the table — only to hastily desist in acute embarrassment at an authoritarian "No points — no Ryvita!" from the landlady. I had been home for half-term, and my ration book had come back empty of 'points' — those little squares of paper.

The war ended when I was half-way through my four-year course. Although the balance of the sexes was fairly soon restored, it was to be a few years before university life and social activities returned to the traditionally carefree atmosphere — if they ever did.

Margaret Forde

PICTURES OF A SOUTH SIDE CHILDHOOD

I remember the 1930s well — what a happy childhood!

I lived in Roxburgh Terrace, South Side. The Roxy Picture House was at the end of the terrace. We kids used to sneak in without paying which was very exciting because the doorman was always on the look out for us. Then, shining a torch on our faces he would throw us out. What fun we had! It was only a penny to get into the pictures, but we had spent our money on two ha'penny mixed bags out of the Wee Man's shop.

Bonfire night was great fun as well. Boys and girls would go as far as Dalkeith Road collecting old tables, chairs and even wardrobes. We must have been strong, but if the girls complained they just got a thumping from the boys. The most important thing, of course, was watching that no other street stole your bonfire goods!

When we heard about sex — from the boys of course — my chum and I decided that our mothers and dads would "never do that" — the King and Queen were also exempt.

I was sad to see Roxburgh Terrace pulled down. My grandchildren seem to be so bored and have to have money to enjoy themselves.

C Loch (maiden name),
Bruntsfield Place,
Edinburgh

HAPPY DAYS

I have read with many feelings of nostalgia the letter titled *Pleasant Memories of the Pleasance.*

I, too, walked down that area a few weeks ago, with many recollections of the years from 1927 to 1936 when I was a student living at No 48, which is still standing, but within a transformed neighbourhood.

Those were the days when the great work of Harry Miller was carried on by Roderick Murchison, and I have vivid memories of story-telling at the foot of the stairs in 'Westie, Middle and Eastie' down Arthur Street. The loss of the church at the corner is hard to accept, but the change in the whole area is to be welcomed.

I wonder if your correspondent's memory has slipped in calling Harry, 'Sir Harry'. We always knew him as the Very Rev J Harry Miller, CBE, DD.

William Stewart
Netherby Road
Edinburgh

124. What was the film that enthralled these youngsters caught in the front rows by our photographer? There's a bit of a mystery about this picture. The file says simply "children in picture house" without saying which one. It was probably taken in February 1955. A Saturday club maybe?

125. There's no doubt where they're coming from — the steamie, of course. Clean washing in the basins, often pushed along on an old pram, a familiar task for generations of Edinburgh women. It was a place of comradeship and gossip as the clothes were battered clean, and any attempts to close a steamie resulted in local protest. But the competition of the washing machine and laundrette saw their demise during the seventies and eighties.